TET OFFENSIVE
1968

EXPLORE HISTORY'S MAJOR CONFLICTS WITH
BATTLE STORY

YPRES 1914–15
WILL FOWLER

978-0-7524-6196-0 £9.99

GALLIPOLI 1915
PETER DOYLE

978-0-7524-6310-0 £9.99

LOOS 1915
PETER DOYLE

978-0-7524-7933-0 £9.99

CAMBRAI 1917
CHRIS McNAB

978-0-7524-7977-4 £9.99

TOBRUK 1941
PIER PAOLO BATTISTELLI

978-0-7524-6878-5 £9.99

EL ALAMEIN 1942
PIER PAOLO BATTISTELLI

978-0-7524-6202-8 £9.99

ARNHEM 1944
CHRIS BROWN

978-0-7524-6311-7 £9.99

IWO JIMA 1945
ANDREW RAWSON

978-0-7524-6576-0 £9.99

GOOSE GREEN 1982
GREGORY FREMONT-BARNES

978-0-7524-8802-8 £9.99

Visit our website and discover thousands of
other History Press books.
www.thehistorypress.co.uk

TET OFFENSIVE
1968

ANDREW RAWSON

First published 2013 by
Spellmount, an imprint of
The History Press
The Mill, Brimscombe Port
Stroud, Gloucestershire, GL5 2QG
www.thehistorypress.co.uk

© The History Press, 2013

The right of Andrew Rawson to be identified as the Author
of this work has been asserted in accordance with the
Copyrights, Designs and Patents Act 1988.

British Library Cataloguing in Publication Data.
A catalogue record for this book is available from the British Library.

ISBN 978 0 7524 8784 7

Typesetting and origination by The History Press
Printed in Great Britain
Manufacturing managed by Jellyfish Solutions Ltd

CONTENTS

INTRODUCTION

By the end of January 1968, American troops had been fighting in South Vietnam for almost three years. This was, however, part of a much longer war, which had been rumbling along since the end of the Second World War.

Most towns and hamlets were under Viet Cong control, while the South Vietnamese government was on the verge of collapse when the first US Marines came ashore in March 1965. The US military set about establishing bases across the country, driving the Viet Cong from its 'sanctuaries' (safe areas) and helping the South Vietnamese armed forces to restore law and order. All the while, General William C. Westmoreland reassured the American politicians and press that progress was being made and that the war could be won.

By the end of 1968 there were 485,000 US troops based in South Vietnam and they had brought two-thirds of the country's population centres under government control. The number of North Vietnamese and Viet Cong troops in the country was estimated at only 220,000, while 81,000 had been reported killed in 1967. Communist recruitment in the villages was also falling, while the number of men moving down the Ho Chi Minh Trail, the route connecting North and South Vietnam via Laos and Cambodia, had been considerably reduced.

US ground troops had been engaged in military operations across South Vietnam for nearly three years by the beginning of 1968. (NARA-111-CCV-362)

While the American public were weary of the war, the military was promising that improvements were being made and Westmoreland was predicting that it would be over by 1970. However, progress had to be consistent or the people and the politicians would lose confidence in his predictions. Westmoreland stated that the war was entering a new phase in November 1967: 'when the end begins to come into view'. Other agencies supported his view and both the politicians and public were appeased.

Hanoi had other ideas; it was planning to counterattack multiple targets across South Vietnam. It aimed to infiltrate towns and cities ahead of widespread attacks against government buildings and military installations. But military action was the beginning; the catalyst which would start a people's revolution and overthrow the Saigon government.

The plan would start with the North Vietnamese Army (NVA) overrunning Khe Sanh combat base near the border of North Vietnam, recreating the Viet Minh's 1954 victory against the French at Dien Bien Phu. The Viet Cong (VC) would make the initial attacks in all but the north of the country, while the NVA would exploit the chaos.

As 31 January 1968, the Vietnamese New Year and the Year of the Monkey, approached, Military Assistance Command, Vietnam (MACV), the United States' command for all military forces in South Vietnam, knew that the NVA and the Viet Cong were planning attacks to coincide with the celebrations, but they did not know where. They also had no idea about the strength or ferocity of what was about to be unleashed.

The helicopter changed the face of tactical operations in what was a war without frontlines and where the enemy often looked the same as the civilian. (NARA-111-CCV-97)

After 20 January, the eyes of the Free World focused on the NVA attacks against Khe Sanh combat base, near the Demilitarized Zone (DMZ). However, over the days that followed, tens of thousands of NVA and Viet Cong soldiers covertly moved into position. They crawled through tunnels and mingled with the holiday crowds to reach their assembly points in towns and cities across the country, finding arms caches waiting for them.

On 30 and 31 January, the NVA and the Viet Cong attacked dozens of targets across South Vietnam, including government buildings, military installations and cultural targets. Over the days that followed, the world watched the battle unfold on their televisions as United States and South Vietnamese troops fought side by side to regain control of the towns and cities.

While normality was quickly restored in most areas, the damage had been done because the attacks had undermined American support for the war. During those fateful days, the politicians in Washington DC and the rest of the American people had lost faith in their military. General Westmoreland had predicted that the end was about to come into view, and it had; however, it was not the outcome he was hoping for.

Following the Tet Offensive, Westmoreland was replaced by General Creighton W. Abrams. President Lyndon B. Johnson stepped down after poor results in primary elections and was replaced by President Richard Nixon, who had promised 'peace with honour' in the Vietnam War. It was not long before American troops were being withdrawn, giving the

COMBATANTS

2.6 million American servicemen and women served in Southeast Asia: half of them saw combat; over 58,000 were killed; thousands more were wounded; and all of them had been affected. Estimates of the number of Vietnamese men, women and children who died vary from 1 to 3 million.

South Vietnamese armed forces a greater responsibility for operations.

The last American troops left South Vietnam in June 1972, but the struggle continued for another three years. By the spring of 1975, the NVA was ready to enter South Vietnam one more time and the attacks began on 10 March. The South Vietnamese forces were soon overwhelmed and chaos reigned across the country as people tried to escape the advancing Communist troops. On 29 April, President Gerald Ford ordered Operation *Frequent Wind*, the evacuation of American Embassy staff from Saigon. The following day there were chaotic scenes as helicopters flew to the embassy compound while NVA tanks drove through the streets of the city.

TIMELINES

1967

May: Air battles over Hanoi and Haiphong; twenty-six North Vietnamese jets shot down

Late May: US combat units intercept North Vietnamese Army units moving across the Cambodian border and through the Central Highlands

Autumn: 200 officials arrested in Hanoi, removing opposition to the Tet Offensive

1968

Mid-January: Three NVA divisions close in on Khe Sanh, focusing MACV's attention on the security of the combat base

21 January: NVA bombardment of Khe Sanh begins, marking the start of the seventy-nine-day siege. One shell destroys the main ammunition dump, leaving the base dependent on air resupply

24 January: NVA tanks overrun a Laotian Army battalion near Khe Sanh

30 January: Operation *Niagara* sees over 1,000 tons of bombs dropped around Khe Sanh

Beginning of Tet Offensive

30–31 January: Attacks begin in the Da Nang area, twenty-four hours too early. Following early successes, the Allied forces quickly regain control of the situation. US and ARVN troops across the rest of South Vietnam are put on high alert

The Battle for Hue

31 January: During the early hours, the NVA sneak into Hue's Citadel and take control of key installations. Meanwhile, the Viet Cong seize Hue's modern suburbs south of the Perfume River

Tet Offensive 1968

1 February:	ARVN begin clearing Hue Citadel while US Marines start south of the river
10 February:	ARVN troops still struggling to remove the NVA from the Citadel while US Marines have control of the southern suburbs

The Attacks in Saigon

31 January:	Sappers hit key buildings, including the Presidential Palace, the American Embassy and the main radio station. There are also attacks against Tan Son Nhut airbase and Bien Hoa military headquarters in the north of the city
1–4 February:	US troops deploy to regain control of the city streets. The heaviest fighting is in the Cholon district in south-east Saigon

Attacks across the Rest of the Country

31 January:	The Viet Cong attack over a hundred provincial and district capitals. Over the days that follow, US and ARVN troops restore control across the country

The Siege of Khe Sanh Continues

5–8 February:	Attacks resume against the combat base
7 February:	Lang Vei Special Forces Camp is overrun

The Battle for Hue Citadel

10–11 February:	1/5th Marines enter the Citadel
12–21 February:	The Marines fight side by side with the ARVN in a bloody urban battle
22 February:	The Stars and Stripes are hoisted above the Citadel's south-eastern wall
2 March:	Operation *Hue City* ends

Securing Saigon

5–17 February:	Operation *Tran Hung Dao I*, the clearing-up operation across Saigon

1968

1968

Post-Tet Offensive: the Siege of Khe Sanh Ends

30 March	26th Marines strike back, making its first attack since the siege began
1 April:	1st Marines advance along Route 9, at the start of Operation *Pegasus*
8 April:	2/7th Cavalry enter Khe Sanh base, bringing the seventy-nine-day siege to an end

Saigon

17 Feb–28 March:	Operation T*ran Hung Dao I*, the continued clearance of Saigon with scaled down forces
8 March–7 April:	Operation *Quyet Thang* (Resolve to Win), restoring order in Saigon and the surrounding five provinces
16 March:	Massacre of around 400 civilians in My Lai hamlet by troops of the Americal Division. Repercussions immediately felt across the American armed forces and there was outrage across the world when the news broke in 1969
8 April–31 May:	Operation *Toan Thang* (Complete Victory), securing the area around Saigon

The Mini Tet Offensive

5 May:	119 targets attacked across South Vietnam. Many are over in hours
10 – 12 May:	The Battle for Kham Duc Special Forces Camp
12 May:	Mini-Tet Offensive ends
25 May:	Viet Cong attack six pagodas in Saigon; they are quickly stopped
June:	General Westmoreland approves the demolition of Khe Sanh combat base
1 June	Beginning of Operation *Toan Thang II* (Complete Victory II), the continued security of the provinces around Saigon

HISTORICAL BACKGROUND

South Vietnam's Geography and Weather

South Vietnam's varied terrain and seasonal weather affected the nature of warfare waged in the country. While battles were usually fought in rugged mountains, thick jungle, paddy fields or river deltas, a great deal of the fighting during the Tet Offensive took place in urban areas, ranging from the temples in Hue's ancient Citadel to Saigon's poorest suburbs.

South Vietnam can be split into three topographical areas: the Central Highlands, the Central Lowlands north of Saigon, and the Mekong Delta south of the capital. The Central Highlands sit astride South Vietnam's border with Cambodia and Laos, where mountain peaks range from 500–1,000m.

GEOGRAPHY

South Vietnam is long and thin and is never more than 100 miles wide for much of its length. It has over 900 miles of coastline; starting at the Demilitarized Zone, next to the 17th Parallel and the border with North Vietnam, down to the Cambodian border in the Gulf of Siam to the south.

Time after time troops were flown in by helicopter, only to find their adversaries had disappeared. (NARA-111-CCV-93)

The mountains are covered by tropical forests, with some areas covered by multi-canopy trees and elephant grass, and others covered by smaller trees and thick undergrowth. Bamboo thickets, rubber plantations and farms are scattered across the area.

The Central Lowlands is the narrow, heavily populated strip along the coast. The Mekong Delta, south of Saigon, is criss-crossed by rivers, canals and paddy fields. It floods during the monsoon season, leaving most areas underwater.

Temperatures are high all year round, apart from in the mountains along the Laotian border. Humidity is always high and monsoons and tropical cyclones alternatively sweep the northern and the southern regions. An average of nearly 3,000mm of rain falls on Hue between November and February, while Saigon has an average of nearly 1,500mm between June and September.

From French Colonial Rule to Communist Takeover

Resistance fighters fought the Japanese across French Indochina during the Second World War. US Army officers watched when Ho Chi Minh declared Vietnam's independence in September 1945.

THOSE WHO FORGET HISTORY …

Ho Chi Minh never forgot the lessons learned during the Battle of Dien Bien Phu. He hoped to repeat the victory by surrounding the US Marines combat base at Khe Sanh, near the Demilitarized Zone, in January 1968. His plan was to overrun the base, scoring a military and political victory over the Americans.

In August 1950, US advisors set up the Military Assistance Advisory Group, Indochina, in Saigon to control military aid being sent to Southeast Asia.

Ho Chi Minh's troops fought a guerilla war against the French until General Henri Navarre decided to draw them into open battle in November 1953, establishing a base at Dien Bien Phu near the Laotian border. Minh's soldiers occupied the hills surrounding the base and tightened their stranglehold until the French were forced to surrender on 7 May 1954. Two months later, hostilities came to an end and French Indochina was split into two along the 17th Parallel: the Communist north and the Democratic south.

While the French handed over the south to President Ngo Dinh Diem's regime, it became clear that the South Vietnamese armed forces needed assistance to secure the country. In March 1955, more US military advisors arrived in South Vietnam and, eight months later, the Military Assistance Advisory Group, Vietnam, began running training programs.

The United States kept a close eye on developments in Southeast Asia, concerned that if one country came under Communist control, the rest would follow in a theory known as the 'Domino Effect'. Four years of increased violence across South Vietnam were followed by North Vietnam's announcement that it was changing its strategy from a political struggle to an armed struggle. President Dwight D. Eisenhower made the United States' first public commitment to support South Vietnam's fight for independence in April 1959, but the fighting continued and, three months later, two American servicemen were killed during a Viet Cong attack; they would be the first of many.

In 1960, North Vietnam introduced military conscription, sending soldiers to South Vietnam, while the National Liberation Front was established to coordinate the struggle in the south. The beginning of 1961 saw John F. Kennedy elected President of the United States and he pledged additional military assistance at the end of the year in response to a request for help from President Diem.

US Military Assistance Command, Vietnam, was organised in February 1962 to manage the growing American support for the Vietnamese government as it tried to improve national defence and internal security. US field advisors and Special Forces detachments helped to direct South Vietnamese Army operations against the Viet Cong, drawing America deeper into armed conflict. The relocation of thousands of civilians into protected hamlets at the same time proved to be unpopular, creating further difficulties for a government struggling with political turmoil and corruption.

The world's attention centred on Cuba the following October, when America made a stand against the deployment of Soviet missiles close to its shores. The situation ended in a nuclear stand-off between President Kennedy and the USSR's premier, Nikita Khrushchev. Attention returned to South Vietnam on 1 November 1963 when a military coup toppled the government and soldiers executed President Diem. President Kennedy was assassinated in Dallas, Texas, on 22 November 1963, and Lyndon B. Johnson was sworn in.

North Vietnam continued sending troops into South Vietnam, looking to take advantage of the chaos caused by the coup, and the first attacks against US bases were made in July 1964. US Navy ships patrolling off North Vietnam's coast were given permission to shell targets in the Gulf of Tonkin, and the first shots were fired when North Vietnamese patrol boats attacked the destroyer USS *Maddox* on 2 August. Two days later, the North Vietnamese allegedly made a second attack (key witnesses later reported the second attack never took place).

President Johnson immediately ordered retalitory airstrikes against North Vietnamese naval bases, and on 7 August 1964 the US Congress and Senate passed the Tonkin Gulf Resolution, authorising the president to deploy US armed forces to defend the non-Communist nations of Southeast Asia. It meant there was no turning back unless the North Vietnamese backed down; and they had no intention of doing so.

President Johnson was re-elected on 3 November 1964. Two months later, the Viet Cong attacked US military installations and he authorised carrier-based US Navy planes to attack North Vietnam. The attacks escalated into Operation *Rolling Thunder*, the widespread bombing of targets across the country. With the threat against US installations increasing, Johnson gave the order to deploy ground troops; 9th Marine Expeditionary Brigade landed at Da Nang on 8 March 1965, where they were met by government officials and women carrying flower garlands.

Two months later, 173rd Airborne Brigade arrived at Bien Hoa to the north of Saigon, the first US Army unit to deploy. It was the start of an eight-year commitment by US ground troops to South Vietnam; a commitment that would cost tens of thousands of lives, create hundreds of thousands of refugees and change the lives of everyone involved, both soldier and civilian.

The Campaigns, 1965–67

United States military involvement in Southeast Asia began when a small number of advisors were deployed to South Vietnam in March 1962. When the Tet Offensive was launched on 30/31 January 1968, the number of American troops in South Vietnam had increased to nearly half a million. What follows is a brief summary of the increasing conflict between the United States and South Vietnamese troops and their adversaries – the North Vietnamese Army and the Viet Cong – between the spring of 1962 and the end of 1967.

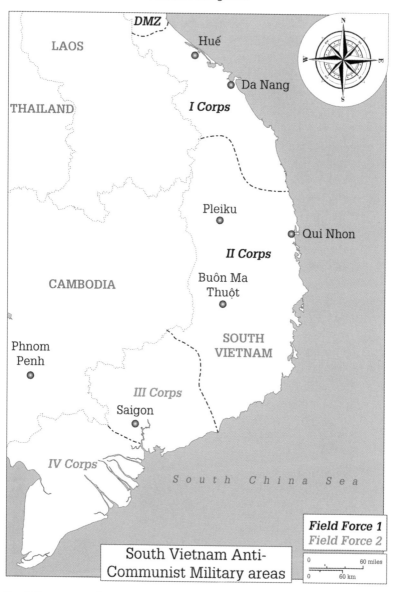

South Vietnam was divided in military areas: I Field Force comprised I and II Corps while II Field Force comprised III and IV Corps.

The first US troops were deployed across South Vietnam in the spring of 1965. The Marine Corps set up I Corps in the north, the US Army took over II and III Corps in the centre, while the ARVN operated in IV Corps across the Mekong Delta. Operations kept the Viet Cong at bay while engineers built bases and ports. An attack against Plei Me, near the Ia Drang Valley, in October was stopped by the 1st Cavalry Division (Airmobile), ending the NVA's attempt to reach Qui Nhon on the coast.

By the end of 1965, US and Allied troops were deployed with III Marine Amphibious Force and South Vietnamese I Corps in the north, I Field Force and South Vietnamese II Corps in the centre, and II Field Force with South Vietnamese III Corps around Saigon. In all areas, search and destroy operations were being made into areas held by the Viet Cong, denying them sanctuaries and limiting their activities.

By March 1966, 3rd Marine Division was deployed along the Demilitarized Zone, stopping North Vietnamese troops crossing into South Vietnam, while B-52s started bombing along the

US soldiers round up Viet Cong suspects for interrogation in an endless war against an elusive enemy. (NARA-111-CCV-401)

US Operations, 1966–67

Between the summers of 1966 and 1967, eighteen large operations, including White Wing/Masher, Hastings, Attleboro and Junction City, were conducted. They drove the Viet Cong from safe areas known as sanctuaries, denying them their traditional hiding places in striking distance of Saigon.

Laotian border in April. In the summer of 1966, the Joint Chiefs of Staff declared their objectives were to defeat the North Vietnamese and Viet Cong while helping the South Vietnamese government take control. But to meet these objectives, ground troops would be forced to fight a costly war of attrition.

By June 1967, nearly 450,000 US servicemen and women had been deployed to Southeast Asia as major operations continued unabated. South Vietnamese armed forces were also conducting their own operations, while their Special Forces were becoming involved in operations in the Central Highlands. North of the Demilitarized Zone, Navy and Air Force planes continued to strike targets across North Vietnam.

THE ARMIES

Tactics

During typical campaigns in the Vietnam War, the US and ARVN armed forces were on the offensive, using their Special Forces units and intelligence leads to locate enemy units before rapidly deploying ground troops by helicopter to trap them. They then called in artillery, helicopter and fixed-wing airstrikes to decimate their enemy. More often than not, though, the Viet Cong were able to hide or slip away, using ambushes and booby traps to disorganise, confuse and delay the US and ARVN troops.

However, the traditional roles were reversed during the Tet Offensive. The NVA and Viet Cong went on the offensive and it was the Free World Forces who had to defend their bases, before deploying and counterattacking.

Free World Forces Tactics

The Americans had been on the offensive for nearly two years when the Tet Offensive began. Operations in the forests and rubber plantations around Saigon and other population centres had driven the Viet Cong from their sanctuaries, often forcing them into the rugged terrain along the border. However, for the first time in the war, the NVA and the Viet Cong came out to fight, forcing the Allied commanders on the defensive; if only for a few days in most cases.

Khe Sanh, near the DMZ, was under siege for seventy-nine days and the Marines had to be on guard around the clock, ready to stop the NVA sappers from breaking into their base. All they could do was dig deeper and use whatever materials they had to hand to create bunkers, shelters and trenches to protect themselves from shells and rockets. Meanwhile, they had to watch while the NVA dug closer and closer. Aerial observers in helicopters and small planes searched for targets while ground sensors and radars monitored troop movements. Equipment designed to detect the ammonia in human sweat and excrement was also used; the machines were known as People Sniffers.

The Marines built thick belts of barbed wire entanglements around their base and installed booby traps, flares and mines to stop the NVA sappers cutting a way through. The NVA usually attacked at night and, when the alarm was raised, it was every man to his position as machine-guns, mortars and artillery hammered the area outside the perimeter wire, and flares lit up the sky.

Elsewhere across South Vietnam, the first the Allies knew about the NVA and Viet Cong intentions was when they emerged from their hiding places to attack. In the first instance, the garrisons of military and government installations had to stand their ground, fighting from prepared positions or risk being overrun. As reports flooded into the headquarters, commanders assessed where the threats were and alerted units so they would be ready to move at daylight.

The Allies often deployed their reserves, using helicopters when possible, on the NVA and Viet Cong lines of communications, aiming to stop reinforcements and supplies getting through. Troops then worked to locate the enemy positions and, often with the help of helicopters, redeployed to surround them. Once the enemy was trapped, artillery and airstrikes were used to destroy them while helicopter gunships swooped low to catch anyone trying to escape the mayhem. The NVA and Viet Cong would split into small groups and make a run for it, hoping to break through the American lines. Helicopters were used to move Allied troops quickly in ever increasing circles to stop them escaping.

In the cities, the Allied units had to cordon off areas and then systematically work their way through them, looking to drive the enemy out; companies attacked blocks, platoons cleared streets and squads assaulted houses in intense urban combat. The Allies could not use their superior firepower because of the threat to civilians and property, and soldiers had to fight with what they could carry: rifles, machine-guns, grenades and small calibre mortars. Tanks were too cumbersome to use in narrow streets and, while the US Army made good use of armoured personnel carriers (APCs) to move troops around, the Marines used the Ontos, a small armoured vehicle mounted with six recoilless rifles, to knock out enemy positions.

Again, the object was to cut the NVA and Viet Cong off from their supplies so they could not prolong the fight. They usually responded by scattering, looking to cause as much trouble as possible with sniper fire and random attacks on buildings such as police stations. The Allies responded by setting up military roadblocks across the town or city, working alongside the National Police to limit enemy movements. At the same time, cordons would be thrown around city blocks while search parties worked their way through to flush out the remaining NVA soldiers and Viet Cong sympathisers. Overall, the aim was to restore law and order as soon as possible before the people lost faith in the government.

The battle for Hue was unique in that the prolonged fighting turned the city into a free fire zone where artillery, helicopters and ships fired into the narrow streets. The Marines devised new tactics to defeat the NVA, using recoilless rifles to blast open buildings and destroy enemy positions. They would then run across the street before the dust settled, conducting a nail biting search of the building, where their enemy might have withdrawn or might be waiting in the shadows. CS gas grenades were sometimes used to debilitate the garrison of a building and the Marines entered wearing gas masks.

NVA and Viet Cong Tactics

Before the Tet Offensive, the NVA and Viet Cong spent most of their time hiding in their jungle camps, waiting for a moment to strike an Allied patrol or fire base. They let the American and South Vietnamese forces go on the offensive, using ambushes to grind them down in a war of attrition.

However, the NVA and Viet Cong launched a large-scale offensive for the first time during the Tet celebrations at the end of January 1968. During the days before the attack, thousands of soldiers were on the move dressed as civilians, assembling just before H-Hour near their objective. Some collected their weapons from concealed arms caches, while others carried theirs hidden

A wide range of captured NVA weaponry, ranging from machine-guns and grenades to rockets and mortars. (NARA-111-CCV-529)

about their body or in carts. No one noticed that there were an unusually high number of funerals around Saigon in the days before Tet; the coffins were filled with arms and ammunition.

Many of the targets chosen by the NVA and Viet Cong were military bases, and they used two methods to inflict the maximum damage. The 'Sapper Attack' involved breaking into a base and then going on the rampage, while the 'Stand Off Attack' involved firing as many missiles as possible at a base.

Allied bases were protected by defensive perimeters comprising an open strip of land covered in barbed wire, mines, trip wires and flares. It was the job of the NVA sappers to breach the perimeter, using stealth to take the garrison by surprise.

In the weeks before Tet, targets were observed from afar while intelligence was gleaned from anyone working inside. While information was being gathered, the sapper commander developed his plan and trained his men.

Each raiding party was divided into two or more assault teams, known as 'arrows', and they were in turn divided into four- or five-man 'cells'. The 'penetration cell' dressed only in shorts and camouflaged their skin with mud, before making the long, slow crawl through the perimeter defences, marking the route with cloth strips. They did not cut the barbed wire entanglements, but used sticks to lift up the barbed wire or mats to cover it so their work would not be discovered.

BANGALORE TORPEDOES

Bangalore torpedoes were a Second World War-era weapon used to blast holes in belts of barbed wire. They were long, thin tubes packed with explosives, and capable of being pushed forward without snagging on the wire. Several tubes were screwed together to form one long 'torpedo', primed and ready to detonate.

Every night they crawled forward, removing mines, disabling trip wires and turning claymore mines around to face the garrison. All the while, mortars fired at the base to drown out noisy activities. As dawn approached, the sappers retraced their route and covered up their tracks.

The plan was to disable a section of the perimeter defences over several nights, until all the booby traps had been removed. Only then would the 'assault cells' move into position, carrying bangalore torpedoes and plastic explosive charges. When the signal was given, they would attack through the weakened perimeter, blasting their way through the final barrier of wire.

Temporary fire bases served troops operating in the field in a war where the control of the population was more important than the control of territory. (NARA-111-CCV-105)

Once inside the perimeter, the sappers opened fire, causing as much confusion as possible. After driving the garrison into their bunkers, they threw their shaped charges inside. While the 'support cells' engaged targets in the open, the assault cells placed demolition charges on chosen targets, such as headquarters bunkers and communications facilities. The explosions would be the sign to withdraw and the support cells would give covering fire while everyone fell back to the assembly point.

By the beginning of 1968, the Allies had built dozens of permanent military bases across South Vietnam, ranging from airfields and heliports to munitions dumps and logistics facilities, and had constructed hundreds of temporary fire bases and supply bases. The government also had many administration buildings to protect.

While the NVA and Viet Cong preferred to breach the defences so they could cause the maximum damage, this was not always possible. Sometimes the defences were too strong or there were insufficient men to carry out an assault. Standoff attacks were the alternative and they were used widely across South Vietnam. Mortars, rockets and recoilless rifles were secretly installed around a base, ready to fire on a given signal in the hope of inflicting damage on the crowded target.

Again, reconnaissance teams observed the base layout, while civilians working inside the base were questioned. At the same time feint attacks were made to assess the defensive measures of the base, and the response times of artillery and helicopters. Local labour also established hidden supply caches close to the launch site.

Only the survey team knew the target location, maximising security, and they were experts at plotting the best launch sites. They calculated the direction to the target and the weapon elevation, and decided whether to use ramps, pits or tripods to support the rocket tubes. The weapon teams would have no time to fire registration rounds and crude devices were used to aim the weapons (bamboo or branches were either stuck in or laid on the ground).

A Viet Cong soldier crouches in his bunker, clutching his AK-47 and waiting for the moment to strike. (NARA-111-CCV-97)

The weapon team was only told about the target as they carried their weapons to the launch site on wooden cradles which could be converted into tripods. The crews arrived after dark and, while some prepared the launch site, wiring their weapons together into batteries, others collected the ammunition. Everything was ready in less than an hour.

Different types of weapons were used for different targets. Indirect fire weapons, such as rockets and mortars, were fired at area targets such as ammunition stores, fuel dumps and airfields. Direct fire weapons, such as recoilless rifles and rocket-propelled grenades, were aimed at bunkers and command centres.

The 57mm and 75mm recoilless rifles were vulnerable because they needed a direct line of fire to the target and they took time to dismantle. Mortars were very popular, but the range of the 60mm version was generally too short, while larger 81/82mm mortars had to be dug in. Rockets were the weapon of choice because they were lightweight, quick to set up and quick to dismantle. They could also deliver a quick, long-range barrage; the 122mm rocket could fire up to 11,000m, nearly twice the range of the 120mm mortar.

William Westmoreland (1914–2005)

Westmoreland graduated as captain from West Point Military Academy in 1936, the highest graduating rank, and he was awarded the Pershing Sword, an award given to the best cadet of the year. After serving as an artillery officer with several commands, he saw combat in the Second World War in Tunisia, Sicily, France and Germany. He was temporary colonel and chief of staff for the 9th Infantry Division after October 1944.

Westmoreland was appointed commander of Military Assistance Command, Vietnam (MACV), in June 1964 and under his command the number of troops in Southeast Asia rose from 16,000 to 535,000. He advocated a war of attrition and repeatedly tried to draw the NVA and Viet Cong into fighting large-scale battles, but they stuck to fighting their guerrilla war. Unable to expand the war into Cambodia and Laos, he was forced to concentrate on improving statistics, making repeated positive assessments of the US military prospects in Vietnam such as: 'We were succeeding. When you looked at specifics, this became a war of attrition. We were winning.'

The battle of Khe Sanh and the Tet Offensive at the beginning of 1968 shook public confidence in Westmoreland's assurances about the war. Even though the NVA and the Viet Cong suffered heavy casualties, leaving the US and South Vietnam in a much stronger military position, the politicians no longer believed his predictions. Fresh political debate and changing public opinion led the Johnson administration to limit further troop deployments and Westmoreland was replaced by General Creighton Abrams in June 1968.

Westmoreland was promoted to Chief of Staff and served in the post until he retired in 1972. He ran unsuccessfully for governor of South Carolina in 1974. In 1986 he served as grand marshall of the Chicago Vietnam Veteran's parade, reuniting the general with his men. General Westmoreland always believed the soldiers under his command deserved better recognition than they received in the United States. He later said, 'I do not believe that the men who served in uniform in Vietnam have been given the credit they deserve. It was a difficult war against an unorthodox enemy.'

General Vo Nguyen Giap (1911–2008)

Giap was awarded a degree in politics, economics and law by the University of Hanoi before becoming a schoolteacher and journalist. As a member of the Communist Party of Vietnam and founder of an underground socialist newspaper, he was forced to flee to China when the French outlawed communism. He joined Ho Chi Minh, leader of the Vietnam Independence League (Viet Minh). After the French authorities executed his family, he returned home in 1944 to help organise resistance against the Japanese.

Sporadic fighting between the Democratic Republic of Vietnam (Viet Minh) and French troops started after the Second World War when France tried to re-establish control. But Giap's moment came in 1954 when his troops surrounded the French base at Dien Bien Phu. After stopping planes from dropping supplies to the base, the attacks began in March and, after fifty-four days, the French surrendered; they had suffered 7,800 casualties and 11,700 soldiers were captured. The French withdrew from French-Indo China soon afterwards.

Giap remained commander in chief of the People's Army of Vietnam, and did so throughout the war against the US, seeing his command expand from a small self-defence force into a large conventional army. Giap was not a supporter of the Tet Offensive and he underwent medical treatment in Hungary while it was being planned, returning when the offensive began. Giap would later state that the Tet Offensive was not only a military strategy, but also one that integrated combat with politics and diplomacy.

In the spring of 1975, Giap's army launched attacks against

Da Nang and Ban Ma Thuot, culminating in the capture of Saigon on 30 April 1975. He was appointed Minister of National Defence in the new government of the Socialist Republic of Vietnam and became Deputy Prime Minister in 1976. He was removed from the Defence Ministry in 1980 and the Politburo in 1982, but remained as DPM until 1991.

The American and ARVN Soldier

Soldiers wore lightweight and loose-fitting jungle fatigues with plenty of pockets over olive-green undershirts and shorts. The hot, humid weather took its toll on uniforms and they soon became faded. Many pockets were difficult to access and personal items were often carried inside the soldier's haversack or tucked in an elastic camouflage band around the helmet.

They wore a steel helmet or tropical hat on their head and lightweight tropical combat boots with canvas-tops on their feet. The boots had cleated soles to give protection against punji stakes. Soldiers were issued with torso body armour, but they were unpopular due to their weight. The US Army issued the M1952 Fragmentation Protective Body Armour while Marines wore the M1955 Armored Vest.

In 1968 soldiers displayed a mixture of old colour and new olive and black unit patches. Ranks were displayed as old insignia on the arm or new black collar pin badges. Helmet covers, tropical hats and flak vests were often covered in personal graffiti.

Some Marines were armed with the M-14 semi-automatic rifle which fired a 7.62mm round; the M14A1 variant had grips and

A young GI is loaded down by a radio, weapons and personal equipment. (NARA-111-CCV-51)

a folding bipod so it could to be used as a light machine-gun. However, most troops were armed with the M16A1 Rifle, a lighter weapon that fired a 5.56mm round, which allowed men to carry more rounds. A selector allowed the soldier to switch between automatic and semi-automatic fire.

Some ARVN units were still armed with obsolete single shot M1 Rifles and semi-automatic M2 Carbines. They were the standard weapons of the Regional Forces, Popular Forces and Civilian Irregular Defense Group (CIDG) troops. A few Special Forces soldiers were armed with the M3A1 Submachine Gun and, occasionally, troops would be armed with the XM177E2 5.56mm Commando Submachine Gun. Officers were armed with the M1911A1 .45 calibre Automatic Pistol, while the rank and file were armed with the M3 knife

The majority of grenades were fragmentation, or 'frag', grenades which exploded in a shower of metal fragments. They came in Lemon or Ball shapes, in heavy and light versions, and in delay and impact versions. The M8 grenade produced white smoke, providing cover while moving across open ground. The M18 grenade produced coloured smoke, creating markers for helicopters collecting casualties and delivering ammunition. The M7 Riot Grenade produced the irritant CS gas and white phosphorous grenades produced a chemical smoke as they burned at a high temperature.

NVA and Viet Cong Soldiers

The People's Army of Vietnam (PAVN) or North Vietnamese Army (NVA) had been sending advisors south to coordinate Viet Cong activities since 1960. By 1968 a regiment typically controlled each of South Vietnam's provinces, with two regional force battalions and an elite provincial force battalion. The NVA recruited and trained in the North and by 1966 it was training over 95,000 men per year; their length of service covered the duration of the war. The majority walked along the trails and paths through Laos and Cambodia, known as the Ho Chi Minh Trail, before crossing the border into South Vietnam. Endless lines of porters carried everything by hand to supply dumps near the border.

NVA units hid in camps, moving in small units every few days to avoid detection. They were guided to their targets by the Local Force Viet Cong, collecting food and ammunition along the way. Following an attack, they returned to their hidden sanctuaries to regroup.

Sappers were elite units who led many of the attacks on military installations, using secrecy and stealth to break through the

NVA soldiers are coaxed out of their hiding places and into captivity. (NARA-111-SC-647264)

perimeter before going on the rampage. During the Tet Offensive they carried out the high-profile attacks on US installations, many of them suicidal attacks. A sapper headquarters and staff had been established in the spring of 1967 and there was a sapper battalion in most of the NVA Military Regions. Sappers received up to three months of extra training, practising reconnaissance, scouting, camouflage and silent movement. They learnt how to disarm traps, mines and flares, and how to destroy perimeter defences and installations.

The Viet Cong had established military, logistical and political systems in most provinces by the start of 1968, and the decentralised system of command involved district leaders using local knowledge to carry out orders from regional headquarters.

Regional units lived and fought in their local district and they established a network of camps, tunnels, bunkers and supply caches capable of accommodating passing NVA and Main Force units. New tunnels were prepared ahead of the Tet Offensive to hide the influx of troops and supplies. The Viet Cong usually went to ground when US or ARVN units swept their area, but emerged to fight when an opportunity arose or if a supply cache was in danger of being discovered.

While Regional units had little military training and few weapons, they trained the Local Militia Units (Dan Quan Du Kich) and many recruits reinforced the Main Force units during the Tet Offensive. They used propaganda and threats to persuade the population to provide rice, give shelter or pay taxes. They also recruited new members and organised local labour.

Main Force Regulars (Chu Luc-Quan) were young men with combat experience and armed with better weapons. They generally camped in sanctuaries in difficult terrain or near the border and came out to fight when an opportunity presented itself. Each company had a Party commissar and each platoon had a Party cell.

Viet Cong political activists were based in urban areas and they raised support in the slums, gathered intelligence and prepared weapons caches. They provided safe havens for Main Force soldiers during the hours before the Tet Offensive and briefed them before they went into action. When the battle began, they emerged to rally public support, organise demonstrations and round up government supporters for interrogation or execution.

All officers carried pistols, as did some senior NCOs and political officers. While the standard NVA pistol was the Makarov PM 9mm Automatic Pistol, the heavier Soviet Tokarev TT33 7.62mm and Chinese Type-51 and Type-54 copies were also used.

Many of the Viet Cong rank and file were armed with a mixture of old French and Soviet weapons or captured weapons. The weapons of choice would have been the Soviet semi-automatic AK-47 Assault Rifle with its wooden butt stock and curved magazine, or the Chinese copy, the Chicom Type-56 7.62mm Assault Rifle with its folding metal stock. Other semi-automatic weapons were the Simonov 7.62mm Self-Loading Rifle (SKS), the Second World War-era Soviet PPSh-41 7.62mm Submachine Gun and the Chinese Type-50 Submachine Gun.

Women played a major part in the preparations of the NVA and Viet Cong for Tet, working as spies, couriers and, eventually, sometimes becoming fighters.

The Kit

United States and ARVN Equipment

United States and ARVN soldiers could call on a massive range of fire support, ranging from heavy machine-guns, mortars and artillery to helicopter gunships, ground attack planes and strategic bombers. However, restrictions as to where they were allowed to fire, particularly in populated areas where there was a danger to civilians, meant they often had to fight without fire support.

The infantry squad's support weapon was the M60 7.62mm calibre General-Purpose Machine-Gun (GPMG), a weapon that could be mounted on vehicles and helicopters. The M2 .50 and M1919A6 .30 calibre machine-guns were two more vehicle-mounted weapons. Infantry squads were also armed with the single-shot, shoulder-fired weapon, M79 Grenade Launcher, known as the Thumper or Blooper, which could fire high explosive, smoke, CS gas and flare grenades. They were also armed with the M72 66mm Light Anti-tank Weapon (LAW), a single shot rocket launcher. Occasionally they used M2A1-7 flamethrowers but the weight of the fuel made them unwieldy.

While the platoon was armed with the M19 60mm mortar, the company was armed with the M29 81mm mortar and the division had M30 4.2in mortars; the larger versions were usually deployed in fire bases or installations. The 90mm M-67 and the 106mm M40A1 recoilless rifles provided direct support.

Bases were protected by a range of mines, with the most popular being the M18A1 Claymore Anti-Personnel Mine, which could be detonated by a manually operated trigger device or a trip wire. Troops also used the small M-14 and the M-16 Bouncing Betty Anti-Personnel Mines. The M4 Phougas, or Fougasse, was a half-buried steel drum that showered an area with burning napalm when detonated.

Two towed 105mm Howitzers, both with a maximum range of 11,000m, were deployed in Vietnam and, while the M101A1 was a modified Second World War model, the M102 had a lower silhouette and was much lighter, making it easier to move. The M114A1 155mm Howitzer was another modified Second World War gun with a maximum range of 14,600m. While the M108 105mm Howitzer was self-propelled, it was so cumbersome that it was rarely moved; it had a range of 11,500m. The M109 155mm Howitzer was manoeuvrable and had a maximum range of 14,600m. The M110A2 Self-Propelled Howitzer could be armed with either the M107 175mm barrel for long-range fire missions up to 32,700m or, where accuracy was required, the M110 8in barrel for short-range missions up to 16,800m.

Artillery and self-propelled howitzers fired a range of ammunition. High-explosive shells sent out jagged metal fragments in all directions, while the Improved Conventional Munition shell was a cluster bomb unit. A Beehive round covered an area with thousands of tiny darts. Base-Ejection smoke shells produced a cloud of smoke, and white phosphorous (WP or Willie-Peter) showered an area with burning fragments and smoke. Illumination shells were used to light up the night sky.

An artillery shell finds its target, detonating an ammunition dump. (NARA-Marine-A191779)

Crews used a range of fuses to achieve the maximum effect. The Mechanical Fuse detonated after a fixed time, while the Proximity Fuse detonated close to a hard surface and the Quick Fuse detonated when the shell hit the ground. The Delay Fuse was designed to detonate once the shell had buried itself underground and was used against bunkers.

The four-man crew of the M48A3 Patton tank aimed the 90mm main gun with a stereoscopic range finder while a xenon searchlight and infrared fire-control equipment meant they could fight at night. The ARVN used the lightweight M41 Walker

An M48 Patton tank crashes through the undergrowth in search of the Viet Cong. (NARA-111-CCV-51)

Bulldog tank and the four-man crew operated the 76mm main gun. Both tanks were armed with a hull-mounted .30 calibre machine-gun and a cupola-mounted .50 calibre machine-gun for close protection.

The M113 was a lightweight armoured personnel carrier and its low ground pressure allowed it to operate where tanks could not. It was armed with a 12.7mm machine-gun and a 7.62mm machine-gun, and while the A1 version was fuelled with gasoline, the A2 used diesel. The M125A1 was armed with an 81mm mortar, the M106A1 was armed with a 107mm mortar, while the M577 was the command vehicle and the unarmed M548 was a cargo carrier. Upgrade kits included gun shields, pintle mounts and hatch armour, and added an extra .50in machine-gun and two 7.62mm machine-guns.

The Marine Corps used the M50 self-propelled anti-tank vehicle, which was armed with six 106mm recoilless rifles. The M50 was known as the 'Ontos', the Greek word for 'Thing'. The Marine Corps Amphibious Ready Group used a variety of armoured amphibious vehicles to make waterbourne combat assaults and ferry passengers. The Mark 5 Tracked Personnel Landing Vehicle had a three-man crew and carried thirty-four men on land or twenty-five in the water; it was armed with a cupola-mounted .30 machine-gun. There were three variants: a command vehicle, one mounting a 105mm howitzer and a recovery vehicle.

A range of helicopters supported the Allied troops and they were used for a variety of functions. The UH-1D Iroquois utility helicopter carried troops into battle using its machine-guns and rockets as direct fire support; it then moved them around the area of operations. The 'Huey' could be fitted with machine-guns, rocket launchers, a mini-gun, cannons, grenade launchers, guided missiles, CS grenades, flares and mines. It was also used to deliver cargo and evacuate casualties. The Marine Corps also used the unarmed UH-34D Seahorse, which had a high cockpit profile.

Two-seater observation helicopters were used for reconnaissance and to acquire targets. While the OH-6A Cayuse-Loach could be

A UH-1D Huey helicopter loaded with ARVN soldiers heads for a landing zone. (NARA-111-CCV-91)

armed with 7.62mm machine-guns or a mini-gun, and the OH-58A Kiowa could be armed with a mini-gun. The AH-1G Huey Cobra was a purpose-designed attack helicopter armed with a chin-mounted 7.62mm mini-gun and 40mm grenade launcher. It could also carry up to seventy-six 2.75in rockets on its stub wings or a 20mm automatic gun. The Tet Offensive was the Cobra's first major combat test and it performed well.

The CH-47C Chinook transport helicopter could carry over thirty men, a 19,772lb payload or 26,228lb of external cargo, allowing it to carry a 105mm howitzer, complete with its crew and a load of ammunition. Machine-guns could be mounted on the Chinook while the armed version, the ACH-47A, had a variety of 20mm cannons, .50 calibre and 7.62mm machine-guns. The Sikorsky CH-54 Tarhe had a backbone airframe design and it could carry up to 20,760lb. It could carry a detachable pod containing over forty men, a command post, a workshop or a mobile hospital.

The CH-54 was nicknamed the Sky Crane or the Flying Crane. The ARVN sometimes used the smaller CH-34C Choctaw–Sikorsky, which could only carry eighteen men.

Four types of fixed-wing fighter aircraft provided most of the close support for the troops on the ground. The McDonnell F-4 Phantoms could carry up to 16,000lb of ordnance and a variety of rockets, missiles or 20mm cannons. While the US Air Force flew F-4E Phantoms from land based airfields, the US Navy flew F-4J Phantoms from Seventh Fleet's aircraft carriers based at Yankee Station in the South China Sea.

While the Vought F-8J Crusader could only carry 5,000lb of ordnance, it could fly in poor weather; it was also armed with four 20mm cannons. The two-seater Grumman A-6 Intruder carried 15,000lb of ordnance and was equipped with advanced electronic equipment. The Marines relied on the Douglas A-4 Skyhawk, which carried 10,000lb of ordnance and was armed with two 20mm cannons.

The B-52 Stratofortress was a long-range, high-altitude bomber designed to carry nuclear weapons; it was used to carry out low-altitude tactical missions in Vietnam. Modified versions could carry around 60,000lb of ordnance and they often bombed the area around Khe Sanh.

Small, two-seater observation aircraft were used for reconnaissance and observation missions, and while the Cessna O-1 Bird Dog was an unarmed, single-engine plane, the twin-engine Cessna O-2A Skymaster could be armed with a 7.62mm mini-gun and two rockets pods. The three variants of the two-seater OV-1 Mohawk were used for photographic reconnaissance, infrared reconnaissance and electronic surveillance using its Side-Looking Airborne Radar (SLAR). Small utility planes, including the U-1A Otter, the U-6A Beaver, the U-8 Seminole and the U-21A Ute, carried out a variety of communication and transport missions.

Cargo aircraft were used to carry men and equipment from the main airbases to forward airfields. Pilots flying to Khe Sanh usually had to land and take off under fire. The twin-engine C-123B

A B-52 Stratofortress loaded with 750lb bombs crosses the South Vietnamese coast, en route to its target. (NARA-USAF-95230)

Fairchild Providers delivered 23,600lb of cargo to small airfields and they were often used to supply Special Forces camps. The C-123K Provider had twin jet pods and anti-skid brakes. The twin-engine C-7A De Havilland Caribou could carry twenty-six troops, twenty stretchers or over 3 tons of cargo.

NVA and Viet Cong Weapons

Infantry squads were supported by the RPD-7.62mm General-Purpose Machine-Gun, which could fire 150 rounds a minute to an effective range of 800m. The Chinese-made Type-24, 7.92mm Heavy Machine-Guns were usually placed in defensive or anti-aircraft positions and many were mounted on wheels. Machine-gun companies had three platoons divided into around eight squads armed with Soviet 12.7mm machine-guns and captured .50 calibre US machine-guns.

NVA units and Viet Cong were often armed with 40mm rocket launchers and, although they had been designed as an anti-tank weapon with an effective range of 500m, they were used against infantry and helicopters. The RPG-2 and Chicom Type-56 launchers fired a fin-stabilised, rocket-propelled grenade, while the improved RPG-7 and Chicom Type-69 fired a finless projectile. A Rocket Regiment had a reconnaissance company and three rocket battalions typically divided into three rocket companies of 107mm, 122mm and 140mm launchers.

A mortar company was organised into three platoons of between two and six 81 or 82mm mortars; some platoons were armed with recoilless rifles. The Soviet 82mm M-1937 and the Chicom Type-53 copy had a range of 3,000km. Platoons were sometimes armed with 60mm mortars including the French-made Stokes-Brandt 60mm, the US M-2 mortar and the Chinese Type-31.

By 1966 medium artillery regiments armed with Soviet howitzers were deployed along the Demilitarized Zone. 105mm batteries usually had twenty-four guns, while 130mm or 152mm batteries had twelve; smaller 85mm or 100mm pieces were sometimes attached.

THE DAYS
BEFORE BATTLE

The build-up to the Tet Offensive began as early as the autumn of 1967, when NVA troops engaged Allied troops in the border regions and near the Demilitarized Zone. The attacks were designed to draw US units towards the border, leaving the ARVN to protect towns and cities across South Vietnam. The engagements also gave new recruits battle experience which would serve them well a few months later. Many Viet Cong units moved to their deployment areas before the end of the year and began building up their supplies for the offensive. They also used the 1967 Christmas ceasefire to check out their objectives.

WARNING

General Weyand was convinced the intelligence reports indicated an imminent attack on South Vietnam's capital. On 10 January 1968 he convinced General Westmoreland to reinforce the area around the city and over the next three weeks thirteen US manoeuvre battalions reinforced the ARVN troops inside the Saigon Circle. It was a move which would change the course of the imminent battle.

Military Police check for bombs outside the US Embassy in Saigon.

Meanwhile, there was a shift in responsibilities for the Allies when the US military handed over control of Saigon to their South Vietnamese counterparts on 15 December 1967. It left the 5th ARVN Ranger Group in control of the capital; 2nd Battalion, 13th Artillery, was the only American combat unit left inside the city limits.

II Field Force was looking to destroy Viet Cong base camps along the Cambodian border north-west of Saigon, and by the beginning of January Lieutenant General Fredrick C. Weyand had deployed thirty-nine battalions ready to attack them. However, the deployment left only fourteen US and Free World battalions inside the Saigon Circle, a 29-mile zone around the capital.

While the number of contacts along the border fell, II Field Force intelligence was concerned that enemy radio traffic around Saigon was steadily increasing. Something was happening, but no one was quite sure what.

While II Field Force reinforced the Saigon area, Westmoreland was focused on areas south of the Demilitarized Zone.

Intelligence estimates put the number of NVA troops gathering around Khe Sanh alone at anywhere between 20,000 and 40,000. More were gathering along the rest of South Vietnam's border with Laos and Cambodia.

Planning the Tet Offensive

In the past, the Viet Cong had only made night-time hit and run attacks against military and government targets. During the Tet Offensive, however, the tactics changed because they intended to capture key installations and hold them until reinforcements arrived.

Targets included a wide range of government installations, including regional and district headquarters, police buildings and radio stations. They also covered many types of military targets including fire bases, arms dumps, communications centres, airfields and logistics areas. The Military Affairs Committee

This helicopter base in Saigon was one of many targets selected by the Viet Cong. The revetments are designed to contain damage when one of the UH-1D helicopters was hit. (NARA-111-CCV-97)

selected targets in each district and, after gaining the approval of the Province Committee, they delegated the planning to their three staff sections.

The Military Staff sent reconnaissance units out to study the target and the surrounding terrain. Observers watched from afar, making estimates of the defences, troop strengths and the weapons protecting the base. At the same time sappers tried to infiltrate the perimeter to find out more detailed information. The Political Staff questioned the local Viet Cong and villagers about Allied military activity and encouraged (sometimes forcibly) people working inside bases to spy for them. Meanwhile, the Rear Services Staff rounded up civilians to work as labourers, porters, guides or lookouts. They also recruited sympathetic villagers to hide and feed the sappers.

Once all the information had been collected and analysed, the Military Staff submitted their plans to the Military Affairs Committee for approval using the 'One Slow, Four Quick' principle; slow planning, a quick advance, a quick attack, a quick clearance (of equipment and casualties) and a quick withdrawal (to a pre-arranged rendezvous point). The planning was to be slow and deliberate, and officers often used sand tables and models to instruct their men about the target. The advance had to be quick and, while troops marched to their assembly point, sappers cut a way through the base perimeter. A quick attack would take advantage of the confusion caused.

Attacks could now be carried out according to three principles: a strong fight, a strong assault and a strong pursuit. The combination of the three would allow the NVA or Viet Cong to create havoc inside the base. In the past, troops made a quick withdrawal, before the Americans could deploy their superior firepower. They then headed quickly to their rendezvous before dispersing. Only this time many of the targets were in urban areas where the Americans could not use airstrikes, artillery bombardments and helicopter gunships because of the danger to civilians and the risk of heavy collateral damage.

Deploying for Battle

In the weeks and days before the Tet holiday, thousands of soldiers walked hundreds of miles to reach their assembly points. Many started in North Vietnam and marched south along the Ho Chi Minh Trail, passing through Laos and into Cambodia. Once across the South Vietnamese border, they regularly moved at night to avoid detection, each time getting closer to their target. While reconnaissance teams checked routes and questioned villagers, liaison teams organised lookouts, guides, billets and supplies.

Scouts led the way, while the rest of the unit followed in single file, often creating long, drawn-out columns. A rearguard team made sure that no one followed. Movement was dangerous and units often had to make long detours around Allied positions. Local Force Viet Cong had located suitable campsites and prepared tunnels, ammunition caches and food stores.

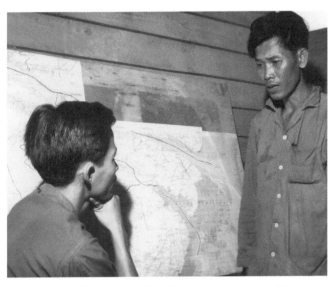

Very few NVA prisoners were taken during the run up to the Tet Offensive. Questioning discovered very little because objectives were only revealed at the last minute. (NARA-111-CCV-97)

The Days Before Battle

PLAYING BY THE RULES

Local Viet Cong units often took advantage of the Allied
Rules of Engagement prohibiting artillery and air attacks
on inhabited areas. Villagers were forced to help build
a new camp during the daytime and then kept under
curfew at night. An outer ring of bunkers was built
outside of the village while the inner defensive belt was
dug under and around the huts.

Camps were often hidden in dense jungle areas where they were difficult to locate but easy to escape from. While billets, classrooms and training areas were built above ground, underground headquarters and hospitals were connected by tunnels. Bunkers had camouflaged roofs protected by logs and earth, while the firing slits served as the exits. Typically, each camp had two or three concentric rings of bunkers connected by trenches. The troops held the outer line during an attack, regrouping on the inner line if necessary, a tactic known as 'rubber banding'.

Digging in, Ready for Battle

While most of the NVA and Viet Cong targets were in the towns and cities, Khe Sanh base, south of the DMZ, was in the middle of nowhere. Here the Marines dug a defensive perimeter around an airstrip while the NVA dug trenches, tunnels and bunkers close to it. The NVA used a mixture of natural materials and discarded items to build fortifications around Khe Sanh base. Bunkers were usually covered by logs held together with a mixture of mud and cement. Sandbags and tin sheeting salvaged from abandoned American positions were treasured items. The NVA dug shallow assault trenches towards the American base, ending in T-shaped fighting positions close to the perimeter. While the assault trenches were left exposed, assembly areas consisting of long lines of small holes to shelter the men were hidden beneath trees or in thick undergrowth.

The line of bunkers and trenches surrounding the Khe Sanh airstrip.
(NARA-Marine-A191629)

There were many observation posts on the hills surrounding the Khe Sanh combat base. Many were protected by a tepee-shaped bunker, made by digging a hole and building a triangular log shelter inside. After backfilling the structure with earth, a camouflaged layer of logs completed the post. Anti-aircraft and mortar positions were dug along supply routes, while larger battery positions were dug on the reverse slopes of the hills surrounding Khe Sanh. Though the mortar gun pits were small and shallow, the aircraft gun pits were deeper and larger. Both were well camouflaged and connected by shallow trenches, while ammunition stores were hidden beneath thick layers of logs and earth.

Tunnels had been used during the war against the French and the old systems were expanded and deepened during the war with the Americans. Each tunnel complex had several camouflaged entrances and many were booby trapped. The tunnels were split into compartments, each with a maze of hidden trapdoors, random turns, hidden side tunnels and dead-ends designed to confuse the intruder. Air shafts, which narrowed to tiny holes on the surface, were dug to ventilate the upper tunnels while

> # THE TUNNELS
>
> Many of the tunnels were less than a metre square; too small for the average American soldier to crawl through. Larger tunnels were dug so that units could move quickly to the frontline, but only a trusted few knew where the hidden trapdoors connecting compartments were. Small rooms with shelving and seating were dug at regular intervals to act as rest rooms.

trapdoors kept the lower levels supplied with fresh air. Water and air locks reduced the effects of concussion from explosions; they also stopped fire and gas spreading.

NVA and Viet Cong Objectives

While Khe Sanh base was being attacked in the north, NVA and Viet Cong units were moving into position all across South Vietnam. In I Corps in the north, the main targets were Quang Tri, Hue, Da Nang, Tam Ky, Chu Lai and Quang Ngai. In II Corps, NVA units would attack Kontum, Pleiku and Ban Me Thuot in the Central Highlands while the Viet Cong targeted the coastal towns of Qui Nhon, Tuy Hoa, Ninh Hoa, Nha Trang and Phan Thiet. There would also be attacks against An Khe, Hau Bon and Da Lat.

North of Saigon attacks would be made against Tay Ninh, Bien Hoa, Phu Coung, Long Binh, Xuan Loc as well as Phuoc Loc to the south-east. General Vo Nguyen Giap wanted to seize eight major objectives inside Saigon to undermine the South Vietnamese government and prepare an uprising. The targets included the Presidential Palace, the American Embassy and key command, control and communications centres across the city. Tan Son Nhut airbase, the MACV command centre, and the ARVN artillery and armour depots at Go Vap were targets in the northern suburbs, while the Chinese suburb of Cholon was a major target to the south.

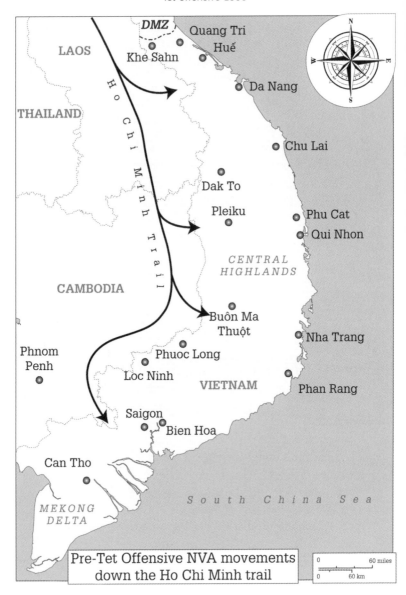

The NVA moved down the Ho Chi Minh Trail to reach key targets before the Tet Offensive.

Viet Cong sappers were tasked with demolishing the Newport Bridge in the north-east suburbs, cutting Highway 1, the main route to the Long Binh logistics centre and the Bien Hoa airbase. II US Field Force and III ARVN Corps command centres were other important targets.

Giap wanted his troops to establish blocking positions around the Saigon perimeter, stopping US reinforcements from entering the city. Some would have to block 25th Infantry Division moving down Route 1 from Chu Chi to the north-west, while others would have to stop 1st Infantry Division using Route 11 from Lai Khe to the north.

By 31 January Giap had thirty-five NVA battalions and two VC divisions in and around Saigon. While MACV knew there had been a great deal of movement over the past few days, they attributed most of it down to the Tet festivities. They knew attacks were imminent but underestimated the scale or the ferocity of those planned across Saigon. Finally, the Viet Cong had many targets in IV Corps and, while Main Force units would attack the provincial capitals across the Mekong Delta, the Local Force units would hit the district capitals.

Allied Intelligence Mistakes

Hindsight is always a wonderful thing and the questions raised over the Tet Offensive are many. What did the Allies know about the NVA and Viet Cong plans and capabilities? What did they know about the timing of the attack and the targets? And what did they do to counter the threats?

Both the Americans and the South Vietnamese had failed to infiltrate either the NVA or the Viet Cong, making it very difficult to predict what their intentions were. Although US intelligence had a good idea of both organisations' Order of Battle and the whereabouts of units, they underestimated their strength at all levels. They underestimated the size of the Main Force and Local Force units by around a third, the size of specialist units by about 50 per cent and the size of administration units by 100 per cent.

A young GI keeps a look out over the sight of his M60 machine-gun. (NARA-111-CCV-97)

They also failed to recognise that many Local Viet Cong soldiers had been drafted into Main Force units to bring them up to strength. They had been replaced by older men of the Self Defence Militia, (the Viet Cong's equivalent of a Home Guard) and boys of Assault Youth units.

Allied intelligence also failed to recognise that South Vietnam's cities and towns were the targets. Security in urban areas, ranging from Saigon and Hue down to provincial and district towns, was controlled by the ARVN and the South Vietnamese police. While it made political sense to let the government control towns and cities, their security arrangements failed to round up the hardcore Viet Cong agents who were preparing for the offensive. Instead, security operations only rounded up large numbers of subsidiary workers. Everyone was taken by surprise when the offensive began, as the following note from a CIA report of the Saigon situation illustrates: 'When Viet Cong regiments surfaced in Saigon, we were astonished. The surprise was unnecessary.'

ALLIED OVERSIGHT

Neither the Self Defence Militia nor Assault Youth had been included on the Allied interpretation of the Order of Battle. Between them they totalled over 100,000 older men and boys, all of them capable of providing support for the thousands of NVA and Viet Cong Main Force soldiers moving into position. It was a serious oversight.

While the police controlled the streets during normal periods, their checkpoints were overwhelmed during the run-up to the Tet holidays when tens of thousands of people were on the move. Many poor people from the slums and rural areas had not been given identification papers, compromising security checks. There were also a lot of false identification papers around, some manufactured and some stolen, allowing NVA and Viet Cong soldiers to reach their assembly points. It did not help that many blank police identification cards had been stolen, undermining the force's integrity.

While the Allied intelligence system in South Vietnam was large, it was also complicated. Information came from a wide range of sources ranging from covert operations, informants, prisoner interrogations and documents captured in the field. A shortage of trained staff and translation complications only added to the problem, leaving the intelligence services suffering from information overload. Over 10,000 documents were being delivered to the Combined Document Exploitation Center every day and the 300 staff had to check to see if each one was worth translating (only around 10 per cent were). Documents were then graded as follows:

Alpha: Intelligence needed in the field; immediately forwarded to the relevant unit
Bravo: Strategically important; translated and summarised for planning operations

Charlie: Low intelligence value; usually filed untranslated,

Delta: Propaganda information; forwarded to psychological warfare (psyops) units

Echo: Communications information, including codes and ciphers

The CIA assessed around 200 reports a day while MACV checked another 600. Both organisations found it difficult to make objective assessments: 'Resisting the temptation to cry wolf every day required judgement and discipline.'

Both Washington and Saigon knew attacks were imminent, and that they would be large ones, but they did not know the timings of the attack nor their objectives. All General Westmoreland could do was to redeploy combat units to protect important installations and then place them on a high state of alert.

On 20 January MACV reported: 'The enemy is presently developing a threatening posture in several areas in order to seek victories essential to achieving prestige and bargaining power. He may exercise his initiatives prior to, during, or after Tet.' On 28 January the CIA reported: 'Within the past week intelligence has provided evidence of a widespread coordinated series of attacks to be launched by the Communists in the near future. Although the bulk of this evidence indicates the most critical areas to be in the northern section of South Vietnam, there are strong indications that key Communist military units throughout most of the country may also be involved. It is not yet possible to determine if the enemy is indeed planning an all-out, country-wide offensive during, or just following, the Tet holiday period.' The following day it stated that 'Reports of a forthcoming "N-Day" have been received from enemy units in all corps areas; they may indicate an increase in activity only, or could mark the beginning of coordinated attacks against allied installations and bases throughout the country. If the latter is the case, it would be the first such coordinated campaign the enemy has attempted. Indications point to "N-Day" being scheduled in the Tet period but it still seems likely that the Communists would wait until after the holiday to carry out a plan.'

So attacks were expected across South Vietnam, but the unanswered question was when. The Vietnamese treated the Tet holiday as Christmas, Thanksgiving and the 4th of July all rolled into one, and most analysts, including General Westmoreland, believed that the attacks would be just before or just after the celebrations.

There were several reasons why the NVA and Viet Cong decided to attack during the holiday period. ARVN forces would be below full strength because many officers and men would be on leave, visiting their families. The large numbers of people on the move also provided cover for thousands of NVA and Viet Cong soldiers moving into cities and towns dressed as civilians. The amount of traffic on the roads also made it easy to move small arms and ammunition into urban areas.

So while the Allies knew an attack was coming and had a rough idea when to expect it, they had underestimated their enemy's capabilities on several levels. They did not believe the Communist propaganda warnings about the offensive nor their plans for a general uprising. They also underestimated the scale of the attacks, the precise targeting of key installations and the coordination between attacks.

On 25 January General Westmoreland cancelled the Tet truce planned for I Corps. Most combat units were prepared for an attack when it came, while many ARVN units cancelled leave, keeping them at full strength. Following premature attacks by Military Region 5 along II Corps' coast on 30 January, units were placed on full alert across the rest of the country. ARVN commanders in the Central Highlands also had an idea of what to expect and many had cancelled leave and placed units on alert.

III Corps was also alerted when the premature attacks were made on 30 January, but Saigon was guarded by ARVN troops and there was no time to move US combat units into the city. Across IV Corps, large numbers of VC were known to be in the towns, but the authorities believed most were visiting their families. The only warning was the alert message on 30 January, too late for the ARVN to prepare or for US manoeuvre battalions to move to the Mekong Delta.

The Opening Rounds at Khe Sanh

Khe Sanh was a military base located close to where the borders of North and South Vietnam met Laos. Although it was isolated, General Westmoreland was determined to hold on to it for many reasons. It secured the western end of the Strong Point Obstacle System, known as the Dyemarker Project (also called the McNamara Line after the US Secretary for Defense, Robert McNamara), a line of strongpoints and electronic detection devices designed to hinder NVA infiltration across the Demilitarized Zone. Khe Sanh combat base and the nearby Special Forces Camp at Lang Vei were also valuable posts for monitoring NVA movement along the Ho Chi Minh Trail across the Laotian border.

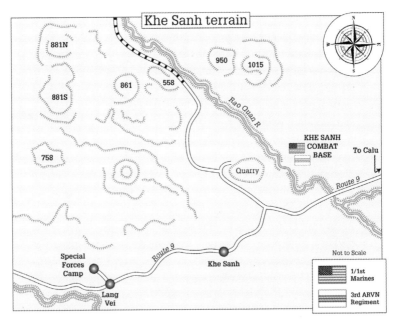

Khe Sanh combat base was surrounded by hills.

Marines return fire with their M60 machine-gun. (NARA-Marine-A190866)

Although the isolated base could be surrounded, leaving it reliant on air resupply, Westmoreland was willing to take the chance in spite of obvious comparisons with the French defeat at Dien Bien Phu at the hands of the Viet Minh in 1954. To abandon the base, or even worse to lose it, would be a propaganda coup for the North Vietnamese and a disaster for the American military.

Khe Sanh combat base was held by the three battalions of the 26th Marines, an artillery battalion and support troops. Three of Colonel David E. Lownds' Marine companies held a large curved perimeter around the airstrip. While 3rd Battalion's Company L held Red Sector at the west end of the airstrip, 1st Battalion's Company C and the rest of Company A held Blue Sector on the north side; and Company B held Gray sector on the south and east sides. The howitzer batteries belonging to 1st Battalion, 15th Marines were dug in along the south side of the airstrip next to the range of support services, including the engineers and motor pool. The Special Operations Group also had a presence on Khe Sanh base and clandestine operations

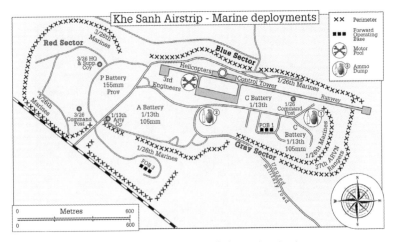

The Marines deployed around the perimeter of Khe Sanh's airstrip.

were coordinated from Forward Operating Base 3 (FOB3), a huge bunker complex adjacent to the southern perimeter.

Outposts had also been established on the hills around Khe Sanh. While Company I and Company M occupied Hill 881 South 7km to the north-west, Company K held Hill 861 another 3km to the east. 2nd Battalion was dug in on Hill 558, 1km east of Hill 861 and Company A's 2nd Platoon guarded the all important radio relay site on Hill 950, 4km north of the combat base.

Combined Action Platoon Oscar and the 915th Regional Force Company were based in Khe Sanh village, 0.5km to the south, where they worked alongside an MACV advisory team. 6.5km to the west of the village was Lang Vei Camp on Route 9, where US Special Forces troops were working with local Bru Montagnard tribesmen under the Civil Irregular Defense Group program. The base was less than 1km from the Laos border.

General Robert E. Cushman wanted to improve Khe Sanh base, but materials were in short supply and the Marines had to do the best they could with what they had to hand. Belts of barbed wire, some over 20m thick, were erected, mines were buried, flares were fixed and booby traps set. In many sectors oil drums were half buried and primed with plastic explosive. They were then filled with Fougasse, the deadly mixture of gasoline and diesel fuel mentioned earlier, which engulfed anyone in reach with a sheet of flame when detonated.

General Westmoreland also arranged reinforcements and both the 1st Brigade, 101st Airborne Division and the 3rd Brigade, 1st Cavalry Division (Airmobile) were on twenty-four-hour standby, ready to fly to the camp. 5th Marine Division also relocated its heavy artillery to boost support for the base while Westmoreland arranged the maximum support from Boeing B-52 Stratofortress heavy bombers. Khe Sanh base was also stocked with thirty days of ammunition so it would not be reliant on immediate air resupply.

On 20 January an NVA officer, Lieutenant La Thanh Tonc, surrendered to the Marines and freely answered questions. He warned of a large attack, the biggest attack since the US had been involved in the war, and he said it would all happen before the Tet celebrations. He stated that 325C NVA Division had orders to capture Quang Tri Province and while 5/95C Regiment was tasked with capturing Hill 1015, 6/95C Regiment would seize Hill 861. 4/95C Regiment would then attack the west end of the airstrip while 101D Regiment attacked the east end. The officer confirmed what Westmoreland already knew, the NVA planned to overrun Khe Sanh, but he still did not know the date. He did not have to wait long. The first assault began later that evening.

The NVA attacked the eight-man Marine reconnaissance team on Hill 689 after dusk and only withdrew after 2,200 rounds of artillery fire had hammered the slopes around the outpost. Shortly after midnight, two red signal flares lit the sky, signalling the start of a full scale attack on Hill 861. Sappers used bangalore torpedoes to blast holes in the wire around the outpost and 500 soldiers filtered through the gaps, overrunning many of Company K's trenches. Although Captain Norman Jasper was wounded, Lieutenant Jerry N. Saulsbury rallied the survivors while hundreds of artillery and mortar rounds hit the slopes around Company K. As the weather closed in, the Marines refused to give up and

Rockets hit Khe Sanh base, showering the surrounding area with smoke and dust. (NARA-Marine-A190594)

the NVA withdrew before dawn, leaving Company K holding the important position.

As Hill 861 quietened down, NVA artillery, mortars and rockets of all calibres hit Khe Sanh combat base. Within minutes Ammunition Supply Point Number 1, near the east end of the runway, was hit and the base was rocked as over 1,500 tons of ammunition began to explode. The Marines dived for cover as fragments and shell cases showered the base while CS gas filled the air. The heat made it impossible to fight the fire and explosions on the burning dump rocked the base for several hours. The climax was an earth-shattering roar as a large quantity of C-4 and other explosives detonated. It left Khe Sanh base short of many types of ammunition, creating a huge logistical headache; one which would trouble the base for weeks to come. As the shelling died down, the Marines were kept on full alert and ready for the NVA attack. It never materialised and when a group of thirty-five NVA soldiers probed the western perimeter later that evening, they were shot down in the wire.

Damage assessments were made during the lull in the bombardment and they were not good. It had destroyed bunkers, field telephone lines, weather monitoring devices and a wide range of other important equipment. However, the damage to the airstrip was the main cause of concern. Shells had ripped apart the steel-planked runway and only 600m out of 1,950m were usable; a part of the airstrip night lighting system had also been damaged. They would have to be repaired before large-capacity cargo aircraft could land.

Although the runway was damaged, ammunition was running low and six Fairchild C-123 Providers, light cargo aircraft of the 315th Air Commando Wing, were ordered to fly to the base. Artillery illumination shells lit up the landing strip as the pilots made the difficult landing, delivering 26 tons of vital ammunition to the Marines. A Sikorsky CH-53 Sea Stallion helicopter also delivered medical supplies for the forty-three wounded Marines; another fourteen had been killed.

While Khe Sanh base was being shelled, the NVA attacked Combined Action Oscar Platoon and Regional Force troops in the village to the south. During the early hours of the 21st, 66th Regiment, 304th NVA Division, attacked the district headquarters where the four-man advisory team and their two Regional Force

A C-130 brings troops and supplies to Khe Sanh, while the airstrip is straddled by mortar rounds. (NARA-Marine-A190615)

platoons fought alongside the two Combined Action Platoons. They held onto the compound and helicopters delivered supplies when the attacks subsided at dawn.

A platoon of 1st Battalion, 26th Marines tried to reach the village but it was forced to turn back. A second attempt ended in disaster when 282nd Assault Helicopter Company delivered 256th Regional Forces Company to the wrong airstrip, finding the NVA waiting for them: twenty-five American pilots and crew and seventy Regional Forces troops were killed in the crossfire.

After a tense night, the controversial decision to evacuate the Americans from Khe Sanh village, leaving the Vietnamese and Montagnards behind, was taken. The evacuation was completed successfully amid frantic scenes on the landing zone, but the commander of the advisory team, Captain Bruce B.G. Clarke, refused to leave his men and led them on foot to Khe Sanh base.

22 January was a busy day for both sides as the siege settled into a routine. Twenty C-123s delivered 130 tons of ammunition and evacuated dozens of wounded without incident, but a CH-46 helicopter was hit during take off, crashing into the perimeter. Lieutenant Colonel John E. Mitchell's 1st Battalion, 9th Marines was ordered to reinforce Khe Sanh base and the headquarters company and two rifle companies landed under fire during the afternoon. With nowhere safe to deploy, the Marines spread out in the perimeter trenches to await further orders.

While the Marines were kept busy digging in and unloading ammunition, artillery and mortar shells bracketed the airstrip while rockets and small arms fire hit the perimeter. Airstrikes against the hills around the base completed the cacophony and destruction around Khe Sanh base.

The following morning Colonel Lownds ordered Colonel Mitchell to extend the western perimeter around a hill and a quarry. The new arrivals secured Red sector, the weakest point in the Khe Sanh perimeter, while Company A's 1st Platoon established an outpost on a small hill called Alpha 1. As the Marines continued to dig deep, the NVA set up new anti-aircraft guns on the flight path, targeting the helicopters and cargo aircraft as they landed and took off. It was a worrying development because the Marines depended on air resupply and on 23 January the guns downed a helicopter and a fighter aircraft in a frantic twenty-minute period.

While 3rd Marine Division's air observers flew regular air patrols during daylight hours, it was difficult to spot the NVA artillery because many guns were concealed by the jungle canopy on the reverse slopes of the hills. Some believed that many heavy guns were hidden in tunnels dug into Co Roc Mountain, a precipitous cliff, across the Laotian border, south-west of the combat base. As the mountain was out of range, B-52s carried out covert bombing strikes to try and knock out the guns. One of the biggest threats was a number of batteries of 122mm Soviet type rockets dug in west of the base. The Marine outpost on Hill 881 South often watched the rockets soaring overhead and gave the base a last minute warning.

On the morning of 24 January, there was another serious development when NVA tanks overran a Laotian Army battalion at

A Marine dives for cover during a rocket attack on Khe Sanh base. (NARA-Marine-A191629)

Ban Houaysan, just across the border; it was only a few kilometres from Khe Sanh. MiG aircraft were also sighted less than 30km west of the base. Meanwhile, on the ground ,the only attack made was against an outpost of Company F, 26th Marines to the north of Hill 558. And so the pattern developed as the Marines dug deeper and the NVA probed closer.

General Westmoreland wanted South Vietnamese units moved to Khe Sanh to give the ARVN a part in the battle. Lieutenant General Hoang Xuan Lam, I Corps commander, agreed and, on 27 January, ARVN 37th Ranger Battalion arrived and dug in at the east end of the runway.

The devastating effects of saturation bombing by B-52s.
(NARA-95286-USAF)

Although the Marines rarely saw the NVA sappers at night, they often found evidence of their activity during morning patrols. They found cut barbed wire camouflaged to look as if it was intact and they found Claymore mines turned round to face the Marine trenches. Even tunnelling was heard and while countermines were dug, no tunnels were found.

One saying in South Vietnam was that 'the night belonged to Charlie' and it was true at Khe Sanh. While helicopter observers stopped the NVA moving during the daytime, they were free to go where they pleased when it was dark. To help the Marines keep track of movements, aircraft dropped sensors that buried themselves in the ground. They recorded vibrations, reporting the approximate size of an NVA unit and the direction and speed of its march. Artillery and mortar crews could then anticipate where to fire for maximum effect.

As the end of January approached, the sensors recorded an incredible build-up in traffic as the hills around Khe Sanh came alive with activity. Major General Rathven McC. Tompkins, commander of the 3rd Marine Division, was concerned that patrols could get cut off and he ordered Lownds to limit them to within 500m of the perimeter.

While the ceasefire for the Tet holiday was scheduled to start at 1.00pm on 29 January, 37th ARVN Ranger Battalion received an unusual radio message two hours before. The NVA had an ARVN Ranger patrol in sight, but it promised not to fire because of the holiday; the radio operator also advised the Rangers to recall their patrols until after the holidays. The patrol was withdrawn immediately and the ARVN unit changed radio frequencies. Later that day, 3rd Marine Division notified Khe Sanh garrison that the Tet truce was cancelled; there was too just much enemy activity.

The air campaign codenamed Operation *Niagara* resumed on 30 January when B-52s dropped a massive 1,125 tons of bombs on the hills around Khe Sanh. Everyone from the commanders on the ground right up to President Johnson was concerned about the base. Some would later criticise them for being fixated

NUCLEAR WEAPONS

President Johnson asked the Chairman of the Joint Chiefs of Staff, General Earle G. Wheeler, if tactical nuclear weapons could be used around Khe Sanh. A secret study group, nicknamed Operation *Fracture Jaw*, carried out a feasibility study and it assessed that civilian casualties would be minimal. Fortunately, the study never went further than the planning stage.

on the situation near the DMZ at the expense of what was happening across the rest of South Vietnam. After asking General Westmoreland for his personal assessment of the Khe Sanh situation, President Johnson circulated it amongst the Service Chiefs of Staff for their comment; they unanimously endorsed it.

Premature Attacks

While secrecy is essential for planning a successful military operation, in General Giap's case it created as many problems as advantages. While instructions to prepare for the offensive were sent out to units in the field, the objectives and timings were kept secret until the last moment. On 29 January officials in Hanoi ordered their front headquarters to delay the attack for twenty-four hours after realising that their lunar calendar was one day out of sync with the calendar used in the south. Some units in Military Region 5, covering I Corps and part of II Corps, either did not receive the instructions or went ahead with the assault because their troops were in exposed positions.

During the early hours of 30 January, thirty Viet Cong units attacked Da Nang, Pleiku, Nha Trang and nine other towns in the northern part of South Vietnam. US intelligence had warned of a countrywide offensive and the localised attacks warned the intelligence chief, Brigadier General Phillip B. Davidson, to expect many more attacks the next day. General Westmoreland cancelled the Tet ceasefire and put garrisons across the remainder of the country on full alert. Combat units were also deployed to blocking positions around Saigon and the large military complexes at Long Bin and Bien Hoa.

The attacks began as expected across South Vietnam during the early hours of 31 January and by the end of the day battles were being fought in five out of six cities, thirty-six out of forty-four provincial capitals, and sixty-four out of 245 district capitals. In many cases the assault troops found the Allied soldiers waiting for them. While the Tet Offensive had not been the complete surprise Giap had hoped for, his ultimate objective would remain a mystery for some time. At a press conference late on 31 January General Westmoreland stated that the attacks on urban areas were diversions for the NVA's main effort against Khe Sanh and along the DMZ. This was plain wrong. The Communists wanted to seize control of urban areas to undermine the people's support for the South Vietnamese government.

What happened when the NVA and the Viet Cong attacked?

THE BATTLEFIELD:
WHAT ACTUALLY HAPPENED?

The Battle for Quang Tri

Quang Tri Province was the northernmost province in South Vietnam, bordering the DMZ, and the town of the same name was a key centre in I Corps. During the early hours of 31 January a single platoon of the 10th Sapper Battalion attacked, alerting the ARVN troops manning Quang Tri's defences. Two battalions of 1st ARVN Regiment were deployed north and north-west of the town while 9th ARVN Airborne Battalion deployed to the east. The rest of 812th NVA Regiment was delayed by flooded streams, but they forced all three ARVN battalions back into the town when they attacked two hours later.

1st Brigade, 1st Cavalry Division was deployed south and west of Quang Tri and Colonel Donald V. Rattan chose to land his troops on the NVA's supply routes. In the late afternoon, 1/12th Cavalry's Company B led the air assault, landing east of Quang Tri. Company C followed, landing in the middle of an enemy heavy weapons unit, fighting for their lives while helicopter gunships circled overhead. The NVA battalion eventually withdrew.

1/5th Cavalry followed, landing two companies in the middle of a second NVA battalion, south-east of Quang Tri. The NVA were taken by surprise and they soon broke contact, using

A platoon advances rapidly across a paddy field as it closes in on an NVA position. (NARA-111-CCV-377)

refugees to cover their withdrawal. While sporadic fighting continued into the night, the battle had been won by Rattan's bold use of his helicopters.

Quang Tri was clear by the following afternoon but 1st Brigade went on the pursuit, looking to hunt down 812th NVA Regiment before it could escape. Many were trapped as 1st Brigade moved in ever-increasing concentric circles, with helicopters leap-frogging troops ahead of the escaping NVA. By the time Rattan closed down the operation, over 900 NVA soldiers had been killed and more than eighty had been captured.

The Battle for Da Nang

During the days before Tet, Colonel Ross R. Miner's 7th Marines had noticed that the contacts around Da Nang were 'increasing in frequency and ferocity; the Viet Cong were seen to be probing their defences. Infrared detectors and XM-3 People Sniffers mounted on helicopters reported strong troop concentrations in the hills west of Da Nang. Patrols also noted that booby traps were being removed, a sure sign new enemy units were moving into the area. The G-2 intelligence officer stated, 'They are finally coming out to fight. We don't know why, but we know they are!' Captured documents confirmed that an attack was imminent and they even stated when it would start.

2nd NVA Division moved onto Go Noi Island on the Thu Bon River, 15km south of Da Nang, while rocket launchers deployed west and north-west of the city. The plan was for two attacks, with an overland one to capture I Corps headquarters and a waterborne one to knock out the bridge between Da Nang and the Tien Cha Peninsula north-east of the city. A rocket bombardment would follow before the Main Force units made their move. Meanwhile, Viet Cong units in Da Nang would force the people to demonstrate, causing chaos on the streets.

Shortly before midnight on 29 January, 1st Marine Division was on standby when 'the alert sounded, and it was all hands to the wire.' Sporadic firing increased in intensity as over a dozen installations were hit by mortars and rockets, with the sound of explosions merging with the Tet fireworks. The bombardment continued until dawn, but while material losses were high, there were few casualties. Five aircraft on Da Nang airbase were destroyed and another fourteen were damaged.

The first attacks were made against the two main bridges connecting Da Nang with the surrounding countryside. Demolition teams were stopped from reaching Tien Cha Bridge

XM People Sniffer

While the XM People Sniffer traced the ammonia in human sweat, urine and waste, it could not distinguish between the enemies and civilians. While it could trace where the enemy was hiding, it sometimes confused human and animal concentrations. The XM-2 was a backpack version while the XM-3 was a helicopter-mounted version.

The remains of a Chinook helicopter after being hit by a rocket. (NARA-111-CCV-147)

and the bridge carrying Route 1 over the Cu De River, north of Da Nang. A later Viet Cong attempt to reach the main Da Nang Bridge on sampans was also stopped.

At 2.50am sappers penetrated the perimeter of the command post of Southern Sector Defense, just north of the Cau Do River. Although they entered the Communications Support Company area, they were driven out before causing too much damage. The next attack hit the operations centre on Hill 200 and the communications bunker was destroyed.

R-20th and 25th Battalions attacked I Corps headquarters at 3.30am, but General Lam refused to believe that the Viet Cong had the audacity to do so. Four ARVN armoured personnel carriers held the complex while Popular and Regional Force units stopped Viet Cong reinforcements from moving through Hoa Vang village. Reinforcements eventually secured the headquarters and airstrikes eventually dispersed the Viet Cong.

By the end of the day the troops who attacked Hoa Vang had been hemmed in and they escaped by swimming to an island on the river. Helicopters flew in a company of the 3/5th Marines and pinned them down while airstrikes and artillery zeroed in. The trapped troops tried to break out overnight but the following morning eighty-eight men were taken prisoner and another 100 bodies were found on the island. The planes dropped their bombs with pinpoint accuracy on the island and Marine John Gundersen recalled the '... concussion from each bomb shaking my face and eyeballs. The explosions blurred by vision momentarily. Small pieces of shrapnel were falling on us with larger pieces buzzing over my head ... I couldn't imagine anyone escaping such a pounding.'

There was sporadic fighting all around Da Nang throughout the following day. Some NVA units tried unsuccessfully to cut Route 1 where it climbed the Hai Van Pass, north of the city. Other units attacked Dien Ban, the capital of Quang Nam Province, south of the airbase. Viet Cong units captured part of the Chi Long camp, near Hoi An, to the south-east. In all cases the ARVN held its ground, but sporadic fighting continued into the following day.

Military Region 5, the headquarters responsible for the northern part of South Vietnam, also attacked many other targets across the Central Highlands, confirming that Da Nang was not the only target. Two NVA battalions overran large parts

A fuel dump bursts into flames after being hit by Viet Cong mortars. (NARA-111-CCV-456)

of Kontum but airstrikes dispersed the reinforcements, killing over 300. To the south, 22nd ARVN Rangers were on full alert when the NVA sappers attacked in Pleiku. They held onto key locations before counterattacking and driving the enemy out of the town. Further south, in Ban Me Thuot, the MACV compound and airfield were hit by mortar and rocket attacks while sapper attacks were repulsed. On the coast, sappers captured the radio station and the railway station in Qui Nhon while recoilless rifles hit a nearby supply dump, destroying two ammunition stores. South Korean troops would later recapture the radio station while ARVN Special Forces seized the rail station. Further south, two NVA battalions captured both the provincial and sector headquarters in Nha Trang; the town radio station was also taken.

By daylight on 31 January, most of the attacks made by Military Region 5 had run out of steam. In many places the NVA and Viet Cong were on the defensive and the US Army artillery and mortars were targeting pockets of resistance, while the US airplanes and helicopters hit anything moving in the open. The NVA were unable to move reinforcements easily while the US and ARVN could deploy theirs rapidly by helicopter or road.

North of Da Nang, 4th NVA Regiment temporarily closed Route 1 by destroying three bridges and a culvert. Later that night the NVA attacked Hai Van Pass but were unable to overrun the ARVN outposts and withdrew at dawn. On the northern outskirts of Da Nang the NVA failed to destroy Nam O Bridge, so they entered the nearby hamlet and killed the head of the community.

While the NVA attacked all around the city, the Viet Cong had been on the streets, forcing around 500 people to demonstrate outside a Buddhist Pagoda. The plan was that the demonstration would stop the ARVN and National Police restoring order, allowing the NVA to infiltrate the city. As we have seen, each attack had been stopped in its tracks and General Don J. Robertson summed up the Marines' bravery with the words 'Never have so few done so much to so many.'

While there were minor incidents throughout 31 January, MACV was confident that the situation was under control. The problem was what was going to happen next? MACV's intelligence officer, Brigadier General Davidson, 1st Marine Division,

THE SPOOKY GUNSHIP

The Spooky Gunship was a Douglas AC-47D armed with three side-mounted 7.62 miniguns. The crew could fire hundreds of rounds a minute at a 50m elliptical area, with a round hitting each 2.2m square during a three-second burst. The gunship could also fire flares, illuminating an area. The stream of tracers gave the gunship its nickname, Puff the Magic Dragon.

Marines board a UH-34D Seahorse helicopter. (NARA-Marine-127-GVC-41)

reported 'this is going to happen in the rest of the country tonight or tomorrow morning' – and he was right.

There were over thirty incidents around Da Nang during the night of 30/31 January. 31st NVA Regiment ambushed squads from 1/7th and 3/7th Marines near Hill 55 and reinforcements failed to trap the ambushers. Patrols from 1st Marine Division also spotted NVA and Viet Cong troops moving towards Da Nang and in each case they were targeted by artillery. One large group of around 500 seen moving in the hills south of An Hoa was decimated by the combined fire of artillery batteries and a Spooky Gunship. Between them they stopped important reinforcements reaching Da Nang.

During the early hours of 31 January, the attacks around Da Nang were renewed while the attacks across the rest of South Vietnam began in earnest. The city awoke to the sound of yet more mortar strikes during the early hours. They were followed by more attacks, including eighteen against the Marine outposts along Route 1 between Phu Bai and Da Nang.

Meanwhile, a demonstration led by armed men was stopped from reaching Nam O Bridge, so it headed towards Da Nang. Marines and ARVN Rangers closed in on 4th NVA Regiment north of the city, killing over 150 near the Hai Van Pass.

31st NVA Regiment was stopped from crossing the Yen River, south-west of Da Nang. Helicopters had flown Korean Marines south-east of the city, where they fought alongside 51st ARVN Regiment. Although Hoi An was cleared, the NVA counterattacked along the riverbanks, capturing Duy Xuyen, west of the town.

While there was no ground attack against the Chu Lai airfield, the base was hit by sustained mortar and rocket attacks and collateral damage continued to rise; three planes were destroyed, another twenty-one were damaged, one hangar was destroyed and others were damaged; a bomb dump was also hit. While the Da Nang area had been much quieter during the night of 31 January, the night sky was again filled with explosions when two ammunition dumps were hit.

By 1 February the danger around Da Nang had subsided and helicopters were able to fly Marines out into the countryside, dropping them astride NVA supply routes. They prepared ambushes and forced enemy units into the open where airstrikes and artillery destroyed them. Patrols also checked out the areas the rocket units were using, limiting where crews could deploy their weapons. As the days passed, the number of incidents fell rapidly, but the big question was whether this was the lull before a second storm.

On the night of 2/3 February, Da Nang airbase was hit again and one aircraft was destroyed while six more were damaged. There were also reports that 2nd NVA Division was on the move again west of the city. When a Marine patrol ambushed a group of sixty NVA carrying mortars and automatic weapons on the evening of 5 February, the shooting began in earnest. 7th Marines were shelled, mortared and then attacked, and tanks had to be sent in to stop the NVA overrunning the command compound in Duong Lam.

The heaviest attacks hit 3/5th Marines and 4/51st ARVN Battalion along Route 1, particularly 51st ARVN Regiment's base camp and Thanh Quit Bridge south of Da Nang. Two LVTH-6s Amtracs kept the NVA at bay until reinforcements arrived at dawn, killing over 100 when they tried to escape.

While the second wave of attacks had been dealt with, III Marine Amphibious Force (MAF) Commander, General Cushman, was concerned that his troops faced superior numbers of NVA. His fears increased after the Special Forces Camp at Lang Vei, near Khe Sanh combat base, was overrun on the night of 6/7 February. However, General Westmoreland was more concerned by the lack of initiative being shown by General Cushman and General Robertson. He demanded they work together, pooling 1st Marine and 23rd Americal Division's resources to stop 2nd NVA Division reaching Da Nang's vital areas.

Two battalions from the Americal Division were deployed between the Marine positions along Route 1, south of the Cau Do River, and they were soon engaged. The whole of 196th Light Infantry Brigade was in position later that evening under the command of Colonel Louis Gelling. Task Force Miracle, as it was called, stopped further NVA attacks and, by 9 February, 2nd NVA Division was withdrawing, having given up trying to reach Da Nang. Task Force Miracle was then returned to Army command, leaving the Marines to follow up 2nd NVA Division's withdrawal.

During the two-week battle for the Da Nang area, the Marines had suffered 124 killed in action and 480 wounded in action, while 196th Light Infantry Brigade lost eighteen killed and fifty-nine wounded; the ARVN suffered around the same number of casualties. The NVA and Viet Cong suffered about 1,300 casualties and 1st Viet Cong Regiment was hit the hardest, losing around 600 men.

The attack on the Da Nang area exposed several weaknesses in the NVA planning and execution. The commander appeared to have misinterpreted the situation and at times he did not follow his orders. It meant that, even though 2nd NVA Division was delayed, the Viet Cong were not established inside the city when

ARVN Rangers coordinate an attack on a Viet Cong position. (NARA-111-CCV-529)

the attack started. To make matters worse, NVA units always advanced in straight lines to and from their objective, making it easy to counter their moves.

The Battle for Hue Begins

Hue was the former Imperial capital of the Nguyen Lords and by 1968 it was home to 140,000 people. The Perfume River (Huong River) divided the city into two distinct areas. The nineteenth-century Citadel on the north bank was surrounded by three ramparts, forming the Capital Citadel, the Royal Citadel and the Forbidden Citadel. High walls and towers enclose 7.8 square km of houses, market places, gardens and parks. The elegant pagodas and moats surrounding the Imperial Palace complete what was, and still is, a major Vietnamese cultural centre. The modern suburbs were to the south of the Perfume River, covering an area half the size of the Citadel in a triangle formed by the river and the Phu Cam Canal.

Hue had always been a safe place to live and preparations for the Tet celebrations were well underway when the ceasefire was cancelled. The premature attack on Da Nang during the early hours of 31 January put everyone on full alert. 1st AVRN Division was responsible for the Hue area and while all leave was cancelled, in most cases it was too late; many soldiers had already left to join their families.

Brigadier General Ngo Quang Truong only had a few troops inside the Citadel. While his divisional headquarters was situated in the Mang Cau compound at the northern corner, an elite unit called the Black Panthers held Tay Loc airstrip in the centre. US Advisory staff were based in their own compound south of the Perfume River. Two NVA regiments were slated to enter Hue and while 6th NVA Regiment would assault the Citadel, 4th NVA Regiment would attack the modern suburbs; between them they had over 200 targets to capture across the city. They also had the names and addresses of several hundred government officials, workers and sympathisers who were to be rounded up and executed.

While the ceasefire had been cancelled, no one noticed that there were a large number of young men entering the city amongst the crowds. They were the NVA troops and they walked through the Citadel gates dressed as peasants with their uniforms and equipment hidden in knapsacks and carts. Some brought their weapons with them while others collected theirs from concealed caches. They then hid in the shadows, changed into their uniforms, checked their weapons and waited for the signal to attack.

Around midnight, 6th Regiment left its base camp, a few kilometres west of Hue, and marched in three columns towards the Citadel. Although two columns were spotted by a roving ARVN patrol, no action was taken and they continued on their way. As they approached the Citadel gates a flare lit up the sky, marking the start of the attack. It was just after 2.30am on 31 January.

Sappers wearing ARVN uniforms emerged from their hiding places and killed the guards at An Hoa Gate, letting 6th Regiment enter the western corner of the Citadel. 802nd Battalion headed north-east and attacked the 200 guards protecting the Mang Cau compound. Meanwhile, 800th Battalion headed for the airstrip in the centre of the Citadel, coming under heavy fire from the Black Panthers. They captured the runway when General Truong ordered the Panthers to redeploy to his headquarters. NVA platoons fanned out across the Citadel throughout the night and by dawn over half of it, including the Imperial Palace, was occupied. The Viet Cong's red, blue and gold flag was also flying from the 35m-high Flag Tower on the south-east wall.

South of the Perfume River, 4th NVA Regiment and 804th Battalion captured many targets and released many Viet Cong supporters from the prison. The MACV compound was overrun and the staff were trapped inside their hotel.

General Truong needed reinforcements and he needed them fast. 3rd Troop, 7th ARVN Cavalry and 7th Battalion of the ARVN Airborne task force saddled up and headed south along Route 1, not knowing what was ahead. The convoy came under fire 400 metres from the Citadel wall and was unable to get any closer. 2nd ARVN Airborne Battalion helped to overwhelm the roadblock and the two battalions entered the Citadel, having suffered 131 casualties.

2nd and 3rd Battalions of the 3rd ARVN Regiment advanced towards the south-west corner of the Citadel, looking to secure bridges across the Perfume River. They came under fire from the battlements and were forced to dig in in front of the Citadel walls. South-east of the city NVA units surrounded the rest of 3rd ARVN Regiment and, while 1st Battalion escaped along the Perfume River on motorised junks, 4th Battalion was trapped for several days. South of the city 7th ARVN Armored Cavalry Squadron

Eddie Adams' Pulitzer Prize-winning photograph: General Nguyen Ngoc Loan executes Nguyen Van Lem after he was caught killing police officers and civilians.

drove north along Route 1, coming under fire as it crossed the An Cuu Bridge. The squadron crossed the Phu Lam Canal at its second attempt but was stopped by heavy fire from the police headquarters. With their road forward blocked, the ARVN withdrew to await reinforcements.

It was late morning when the first unit of US Marines was on its way from Task Force X-Ray's perimeter where Brigadier General Foster 'Frosty' C. Lahue had three battalions stretched out along Route 1, south of Hue. While 1/5th Marines held the Hai Van Pass, north of Da Nang and 2/5th Marines covered the Phu Loc area, 1/1st Marines held Route 1 immediately south of Hue. The brigade had already been under fire for twenty-four hours as NVA companies attacked Phu Loc town, Phu Bai airstrip and the Truoi River Bridge. 1/1st Marines alone had fended off over fifteen attacks against its position along Route 1.

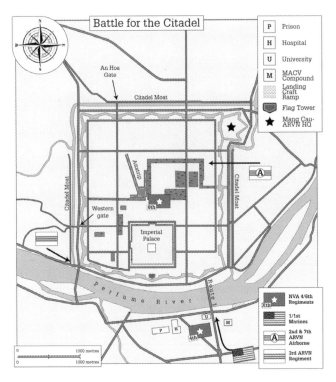

While the ARVN fought to retake Hue's Citadel, the Marines battled south of the river.

When Lahue received the order to reinforce the ARVN in Hue, he ordered 1/1st Marines to mount up on trucks and drive north into Hue. Along the way they commandeered four M48 tanks and a handful of ARVN tanks. The Marines braved sniper fire south of the An Cuu bridge and then came under heavy crossfire on the north side of the canal. Reinforcements in the shape of Company G, 2/5th Marines reached Company A in the early afternoon and together they pushed on to the MACV compound.

As Company A secured the compound, the wounded were loaded onto the trucks and driven back through a gauntlet of fire to get to Phu Bai. Meanwhile, half of the tanks accompanied

A Marine runs for cover with two LAAWs (Light Anti-Tank Weapon) strapped to his back. The barrel of a recoilless rifle can be seen in the background. (NARA-Marine-A190-301)

Company G to the Perfume River, where the plan was to cross the main bridge and fight their way into the Citadel. As Company G crossed the bridge and the M48 tanks gave covering fire, the ARVN tanks refused to help. Two platoons of Marines crossed only to come under heavy fire from the Citadel walls on the north bank. The company commander reluctantly had to call them back, dragging their casualties with them. Over sixty men were killed and injured in the abortive attack and the Marines had to commandeer vehicles to get their wounded to the MACV compound.

By nightfall Hue was firmly in the hands of the NVA. However, as far as General Westmoreland was concerned, there were only three NVA companies in the city and a Marine battalion was fighting alongside the ARVN. While that may have been true, the odds were stacked against the Marines; it would take many more troops to oust the NVA.

On 1 February areas of responsibility were split and, while 1st ARVN Division concentrated on securing the Citadel, Task Force X-Ray focused on clearing the south side of the river. General Lahue, told correspondents: 'Very definitely, we control the south side of the city … I don't think they [the NVA] have any resupply capability and once they use up what they brought in, they're finished.' It was a confident statement, one which would come back to haunt Task Force X-Ray's commander, especially when the 1/1st Marines came under heavy fire from the provincial headquarters and the prison.

Helicopters managed to fly 2/5th Marines' Company F to the south bank of the Perfume River, where it tried in vain to reach the signals unit surrounded by NVA units. Low cloud made it difficult to call in airstrikes and helicopter attacks and it was too dangerous to use artillery strikes in the city streets. It meant that the Marines had to be left to their own devices when they staged attacks.

Inside the Citadel, the Black Panthers helped 2nd and 7th Airborne Battalions to recapture the airfield while 1/3rd Battalion reached the Mang Ca compound. But while Marine helicopters flew in part of 4/2nd Battalion, 2/3rd and 3/3rd Battalions were still pinned down outside the south-west wall.

ROUGH RIDER CONVOYS

Rough Rider convoys were fleets of 2.5-ton and 5-ton lorries fitted with armoured cabs and armed with weapons. Damaged vehicles were cannibalised for spare parts, which were used to turn the lorries into gun trucks. The convoys were able to drive through known ambush areas to deliver supplies to outlying bases.

On 2 February, 3rd Brigade of 1st Cavalry Division (Airmobile) was slated to cut off the NVA supply routes north and west of Hue. Helicopters airlifted 2/12th Cavalry to a landing zone on the south bank of the Song Bo River, 16km north-west of Hue. While 2/12th Cavalry advanced towards the Citadel, 1/7th Cavalry and 3rd Brigade headquarters were flown in.

Low cloud and anti-aircraft fire prevented 2/12th Cavalry from carrying out an air assault on 3 February so it advanced on foot towards the Citadel, coming under heavy fire from Que Chu hamlet. While the Cavalry reached the northern perimeter of the hamlet by nightfall, the NVA were able to reinforce the position under cover of darkness. They then went on the offensive, forcing Lieutenant Colonel Richard S. Sweet's men to move to a safer position 1.2km to the south-west, carrying over sixty casualties with them. The following morning, Lieutenant Colonel James Vaught's 5/7th Cavalry assaulted Que Chu while Sweet's battalion tried to attack from the south; it was stopped by a strong NVA force in Bon Tri hamlet. Both battalions became bogged down in a difficult battle which would last several days; meanwhile, the NVA continued to reinforce the Citadel.

However, there was good news for the Americans south of the river on 2 February where 2/5th Marines relieved the signals crew at the radio station and 1/1st Marines reached the university. Although the railway bridge over the Perfume River had been destroyed during the night, the bridge over the Phu Cam Canal was still intact. When Company H of 2/5th Marines drove across on a Rough Rider convoy, sniper fire triggered friendly fire from the Marines in the MACV compound. Fortunately, there were few casualties and Company H was able to reinforce Company G's perimeter.

On the morning of 3 February, Rough Rider convoys carried the command groups of 1/5th and 2/5th Marines through the rain and fog into Hue. In the words of Lieutenant Colonel Ernest C. Cheatham, 'and so the next morning we went. We went blind. And that was it …' Colonel Stanley Hughes directed Cheatham to move into the university compound, while 2/5th Marines repeatedly attacked the public health offices, the treasury and the postal buildings. In the words of the battalion commander, 'that means mustering everybody's courage and energy up … You'd assault and back you'd come, dragging your wounded and then muster it up again and try again.' The Marines were only able to

The crew of a recoilless rifle aim their weapon at an NVA strongpoint. (NARA-Marine-371216)

M50 SELF-PROPELLED ANTI-TANK VEHICLE (ONTOS)

The Marines found that tanks drew fire and the air was filled with bullets and shells as soon as one edged out into a street. Instead the Ontos, a small, manoeuvrable armoured vehicle, was used to good effect. The peculiar shaped vehicles were armed with six 106mm recoilless rifles and a single round could knock a large hole in a wall up to 500m away.

capture the public health building and were forced to abandon it at dusk so they could secure their perimeter.

1/1st Marines moved up on 2/5th Marines' left flank on the morning of 4 February and attacked the Joan of Arc Church. The NVA were barricaded inside and the Marines had to fire recoilless rifle rounds at the building and move into the cloisters. Sergeant Alfredo Gonzalez knocked out two rocket positions in the adjacent school before he was killed; he was awarded the Medal of Honor.

Meanwhile, 2/5th Marines discovered that smoke attracted lots of NVA fire, making it dangerous to use it to cover movement. Instead they used it to draw fire and then pinpointed enemy positions for the recoilless rifle teams who blasted open walls. The Marines then ran through the clouds of dust, across the streets and dived inside the damaged building. This new tactic allowed the 2/5th Marines to capture the public health building at last. Marines in gas masks also stormed the treasury after filling the building with CS gas.

While Task Force X-Ray was extending its hold over Hue's suburbs, the NVA were pulling out all the stops to cut its lines of communication. Sappers had destroyed the An Cuu bridge during the night, stopping the Rough Rider convoys crossing the Phu Lam Canal. Low cloud and mist created foul flying weather and the Marine helicopters were often forced to fly low through a gauntlet of fire to bring in supplies and evacuate casualties. It was down to the Navy to keep the Task Force supplied and landing craft crews braved heavy fire from the banks of the Perfume River as they delivered food and ammunition to the Marines.

As the hours and days passed, the Marines adapted to street fighting; but it was dangerous work, especially as they were always on the offensive. Urban warfare is confusing and bloody at the best of times, but the lack of accurate maps made it harder to plan attacks.

2/5th Marines had an area eleven blocks wide and nine blocks deep to clear and there were never enough men to go round. There was no room to manoeuvre in the narrow streets and the Marines had to capture a block building by building, without the benefit of air or artillery support; only the 81mm mortars could be relied on for close support.

And so the battle continued. On 5 February 1/1st Marines struggled to advance, but 2/5th Marines entered the hospital grounds and evacuated the patients. The hospital building was cleared the following day and the fight continued around the prison. Although Company G blasted a hole in the wall and threw in CS gas canisters, the NVA garrison threw them straight back out. The fall of the provincial headquarters changed the balance of the battle and the NVA started to withdraw as soon as the Stars and Stripes replaced the Viet Cong flag. The Marines then demolished part of the Le Loi Bridge, stopping the NVA escaping north over the Perfume River and into the Citadel.

For the next four days, 1/1st and 2/5th Marines mopped up the modern suburbs and, by 10 February, 2/1st Marines were crossing the Phu Cam Canal and strengthening the perimeter. While the authorities opened a refugee centre where people could get food and shelter, the police started to take over security, bringing a sense of normality to the smoking suburbs. When the An Cuu bridge reopened on 13 February, lorries started to bring in supplies for soldiers and civilians alike.

Thirty-eight Marines had been killed, while another 320 had been wounded during the ten-day battle. The NVA casualties were harder to calculate, but the number is estimated to be 1,000.

The Battles for Long Binh and Bien Hoa

There were three important bases 21km to the north-east of Saigon: ARVN III Corps headquarters in Bien Hoa; the United States Air Force base on the outskirts of Bien Hoa; and the huge ammunition dump at Long Binh. Following General Westmoreland's cancellation of the ceasefire, 9th Division's 2/47th Infantry (Mechanised) had set up blocking positions around all three. By 5.00am on 31 January, all three bases reported that they were under attack by units of the 5th VC Division. Lieutenant Colonel John B. Tower deployed his three mechanised companies to relieve the garrisons in what would become a confusing number of skirmishes all across the Bien Hoa–Long Binh area.

Company A engaged 275th VC Regiment in Ho Nai village before relieving the garrison of the nearby prisoner-of-war compound on Route 1. Company B made its way to Long Binh ammunition dump, driving out the Viet Cong sappers before they could detonate their satchel charges. Meanwhile, Company C fought its way past 275th VC Regiment astride Highway 1 before stopping 274th VC Regiment's attack on Bien Hoa airbase. It went on to infiltrate Bien Hoa town, breaking up 238th VC Battalion's siege of III Corps' compound. Company C spent the rest of the day engaged in house-to-house fighting and, by nightfall, it had cleared Bien Hoa after having only suffered eight casualties.

While Colonel Tower's men worked their way towards Bien Hoa town, Troop A from 9th Division's 3rd Squadron, 5th Cavalry, drove down Highway 1 towards Bien Hoa airbase. They had to brave the same corridor of fire on the long journey, returning fire as they drove through an ambush in Trang Bom. Although a destroyed bridge stopped most of the tanks reaching their objective, the M113s forded the stream. They reinforced 2/506th Battalion, 101st Airborne Division, which had been fighting since it had been airlifted into the base earlier that morning.

The Viet Cong had wanted to halt planes and helicopters taking off from the airfield, stopping them providing fire support to units

A GI returns fire during an attack on Long Binh base. (NARA-111-CCV-529)

around Saigon. However, the plan to storm the main gate and overrun the helicopter area never materialised. Elsewhere on the base, the Viet Cong tried in vain to storm the bunkers, aiming to turn their heavy machine-guns on the runways. Instead, helicopter gunships helped the troops on the ground clear the east end of the base by nightfall. The battle continued the following day, but the Viet Cong finally disengaged when 11th Armored Cavalry Regiment arrived at dusk. After a difficult thirty-six hours, Bien Hoa airbase was fully operational again.

At first light on 1 February, 1st Infantry Division assembled reaction forces at its bases north of Saigon and were soon heading south along Route 1. The Big Red One was expecting trouble and, when Major General John H. Hay's infantry ran into 273rd VC Regiment's roadblocks, they surrounded Phu Loi while their artillery deployed. For once, the Viet Cong were not going to escape into the jungle and after the howitzers had fired 3,500 rounds at the village, the GIs moved in to mop up the survivors. There were not many; 273rd Regiment had been decimated, leaving the main road to Saigon open.

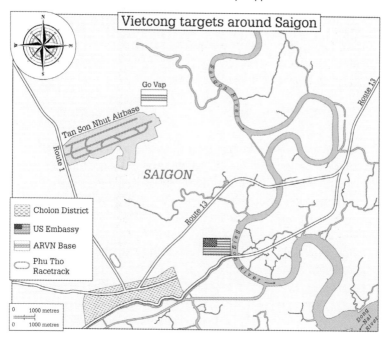

The Viet Cong attacked many targets across Saigon.

The Battle for Saigon

During the early hours of 31 January 1968, Viet Cong troops emerged from their hiding places all over Saigon to attack dozens of targets across the capital. The key ones were the Presidential Palace, the ARVN's Joint General Staff (JGS) compound, the American Embassy, Tan Son Nhut airbase and the Cholon district.

Throughout the night General Weyand listened to incoming reports of enemy contacts in his Tactical Operations Center (TOC) at Long Binh base. He deployed the units under his command to join the ARVN units in the capital and counter the Viet Cong attacks. The widespread nature and scale of the offensive became increasingly apparent as the information was plotted on his operations map. Before dawn, he felt it necessary to order his deputy commander, Major General Keith Ware, into Saigon to take command of the 5,000 American combat troops in action in the city. The attacks happened simultaneously, but the accounts of the main engagements are given in turn.

The Presidential Palace

At 1.30am a platoon from the Viet Cong's C-10 Sapper Battalion attacked Saigon's Presidential Palace. Another platoon tried to break through the gate of the ARVN Joint General Staff compound thirty minutes later. 1st and 2nd VC Local Force Battalions reinforced it when the first attack failed and they eventually broke into the compound. At 4.00am Viet Cong troops ambushed a truck carrying military police of 716th MP Battalion as they headed to an American officers' billet near the JGS headquarters to investigate reports of an attack. Sixteen MPs were killed and twenty-one were wounded in the battle, which lasted all day.

A Viet Cong squad climbed an apartment block and fired down onto the roof of the National Radio station where the

US Ambassador Ellsworth F. Bunker inspects the damage to the American Embassy. (NARA-111-CCV-529)

ARVN guard were sleeping. While the rest of the platoon captured the station, the staff of the transmission station outside the city shut down the radio link, stopping the NVA broadcasting pre-recorded tapes announcing the fall of the Saigon government.

The Attack on the American Embassy

Around 2.30am nineteen sappers from C-10 Sapper Battalion drove to the US Embassy in central Saigon and fired on the two MPs guarding the side gate. They returned fire, locked the gate and reported the attack on their radios, allowing the rest of the guards to secure the perimeter gates. Undeterred, the Viet Cong blew a hole in the perimeter wall. The first two into the compound were shot before the two MPs inside were killed.

Once inside, the Viet Cong fired Type 56s and RPG-2s rockets at the Chancery, blasting several holes in the walls. But their leaders were dead and no one else knew how to use the C-4 explosives they were carrying. They were unable to blast their way inside the Chancery where only three Marines, two Vietnamese and six American civilians were hiding.

The first jeep to respond to the emergency calls was hit by a hail of gunfire as it pulled up outside the Embassy, killing the two MPs inside. The Viet Cong had taken up positions in the Chancery gardens when the Marine Security Guard arrived and they were prepared to fight to the death.

As the gun battle began, Ambassador Ellsworth F. Bunker asked the Saigon police for help, but the police commander wanted American troops to escort his men to the scene. Instead, 716th MP Battalion was ordered to cordon off the Embassy area at around 4.20am. A helicopter carrying 101st Airborne Division paratroopers was forced to abort its landing on the Embassy rooftop due to gunfire. An hour later a medevac helicopter was able to land and it dropped off ammunition (albeit the wrong type) before evacuating a wounded guard.

At first light, MPs shot off the locks of the Embassy's front gate, rammed them open with their jeep and then charged inside the compound. While the surviving Viet Cong were hunted down, a helicopter landed troops from the 101st Airborne Division on the roof and they searched inside the Chancery building. One Viet Cong was shot and wounded as he tried to enter the villa at the rear of the Chancery; the remaining eighteen were shot down in the Embassy gardens.

Although no Viet Cong had entered the Embassy building, by the time the compound had been secured American television stations were reporting that parts of the building had been seized. The news shocked the American public and politicians alike. By the time later reports corrected the facts, many people's minds had been made up about the Tet Offensive.

The Battle for Tan Son Nhut

101st VC Regiment had to enter the ARVN depot at Go Vap on the north side of the city and seize tanks from Phu Dong armoured base and 105mm howitzers from Co Lao artillery base. They would then use them to attack the east end of Tan Son Nhut airbase. However, once inside the Phu Dong base they discovered that the tanks had gone, while the howitzers inside Co Lao base had been disabled. Go Vap depot was retaken when the 4th South Vietnamese Marine Corps Battalion counterattacked a few hours later.

A MIXED GARRISON

Tan Son Nhut garrison included 377th Security Police Squadron, two platoons of the MACV headquarters' guard force, ARVN 52nd Regional Force Battalion, and Vice-President Nguyen Cao Ky's bodyguard. Two companies of the 8th ARVN Airborne Battalion who were waiting for a flight in the terminal also fought to recapture the runway.

Soldiers of the Tan Son Nhut Defence Force take cover while engaging snipers near the airbase perimeter. (NARA-111-CCV-529)

On the evening of 30 January, three battalions of the Viet Cong (the D16, the 267th and one of 271st VC Regiment) infiltrated the Vinatexco textile factory just across Highway 1 from Tan Son Nhut airbase. When it was clear that the promised tanks were not coming from Phu Dong, they left the factory at 3.20am and, while the main group headed for the MACV compound on the west side of the airbase, two smaller groups headed for the north and east gates.

The main group breached the western perimeter and they fought running battles with the base garrison across the runway. Although the garrison was holding its own, a call for reinforcements was put out to 25th Infantry Division based at Cu Chi, 24km to the north-west. 3rd Squadron, 4th Cavalry was nearest and squadron commander Lieutenant Colonel Glenn K. Otis ordered

Captain Leo B. Virant and Troop C to drive down Highway 1. As the armoured column drove through the night, Otis flew overhead in his helicopter, warning his men of Viet Cong ambushes. While one platoon stayed behind to secure Hoc Mon Bridge, the rest of Troop C reached Tan Son Nhut at 6.00am where they drove straight into the rear of the Viet Cong.

Although one third of Virant's vehicles were knocked out by rocket-propelled grenades (RPGs) in the fierce battle that followed, they seriously disrupted the Viet Cong attack. At dawn, Otis ordered his air cavalry troop into action and they flew overhead while Troop B drove down Highway 1. It covered the 48km in less than an hour and was soon fighting alongside Troop C, on the Viet Cong's flank. The combination of crossfire, artillery and air attacks drove the enemy from the airfield and back into the textile mill from where they had started; they were then finished off by airstrikes. 3rd Squadron, 4th Cavalry was awarded the Presidential Unit Citation for helping to save Tan Son Nhut airbase; four men, including Otis, received the Distinguished Service Cross.

The Battle for Cholon

One of the Viet Cong's main objectives was the district of Cholon, on the west bank of the Saigon River, in the south-west suburbs of the city. Around one million people lived in the crowded streets and it was the largest concentration of Chinese in Vietnam. They ran their own community and as few Vietnamese police spoke Chinese, the scale of Communist activity in the suburb was unknown. The Viet Cong aimed to take advantage of the situation and start an uprising.

During the early hours of 31 January, 5th and 6th VC Local Force Battalions emerged from their hiding places onto the streets of Cholon. 6th Battalion seized the Phu Tho racetrack in the centre of the suburb, fortifying the stadiums so helicopters could not land on the large open area. Meanwhile, 5th Battalion fanned out into the narrow streets while Communist political cadres rallied support. They also visited the homes of government officials and ARVN officers, arrested them and, in many cases, executed them.

ARVN Rangers were the first to enter Cholon's narrow streets, but at dawn Company A, 3/7th Battalion, and 199th's Reconnaissance Troop assembled on the edge of the urban sprawl. Brigadier General Robert C. Forbes had orders to secure the Phu Tho racetrack so it could be used as a landing zone for the rest of the battalion.

Company A's convoy drove through the narrow streets, only to be ambushed a few blocks short of its objective. An RPG slammed into the leading M113, while the Viet Cong opened fire from rooftops and upper storey windows. With the road ahead blocked, the GIs had to dismount and fight on foot in a fierce house-to-house battle through the side streets. Block by block, Forbes' men pushed the Viet Cong back to the racecourse where they sought cover on the concrete terraces. It took Company A took all day to clear them and when the news reached Forbes' headquarters, helicopters began airlifting the rest of 3/7th Battalion to the track.

ARVN Rangers regroup during the bitter fighting for Cholon; in front of them are Viet Cong dead. (NARA-111-CCV-529)

The following morning two mechanised companies (B and C) of 9th Division's 2/60th Infantry, and 33rd ARVN Ranger Battalion drove to the centre of Cholon. They used the racetrack as their base of operations as companies fanned out, clearing street after street and block after block. The Viet Cong gave up trying to retake the racetrack and instead dispersed. It was the start of a month of skirmishes and a long reign of terror for the residents of Cholon.

Attacks across II Corps

While the main attacks were made against Quang Tri, Da Nang, Hue and Saigon, the NVA and Viet Cong made over 100 attacks across the rest of the country, the majority being aimed at provincial and district capitals.

The heaviest fighting back in the north of II Corps, Kontum, occurred in the towns in the Central Highlands. We have seen how two battalions occupied Kontum on 30 January and how airstrikes hit the reinforcements, killing 300. We have also heard how Pleiku's base commander put a stop to leave and put his men on full alert, so they repulsed the NVA attacks. To the south in Ban Me Thout the NVA also failed to capture their main objectives, the MACV compound and the airfield.

Across II Corps' Lowlands there were attacks against many of the coastal towns. While 21st NVA Regiment and 70th VC Battalion aimed to capture Tam Ky, 6th ARVN Regiment held its positions and began to drive them out at first light; the town was soon under control. 401st VC Battalion targeted Quang Ngai town and the adjacent airfield, but the attacks were uncoordinated and the ARVN held their positions, keeping control of both. The Allies soon had control of Qui Nhon in Binh Dinh Province, while Phu Cat airbase, 16km to the north-west, was shelled and attacked by sappers. There was only sporadic fighting in the towns of Phu Yen and Tuy Hoa to the south, while the huge base at Cam Ranh Bay was untouched. The main attack along the coast north-east of Saigon was made against Phan Thiet, where two battalions penetrated the outer defences.

Kontum was still contested on 1 February and, while Allied troops held the military compounds, the NVA and Viet Cong were entrenched across the town; it was the same in Ban Me Thout to the south. Meanwhile, an attack on Dalat consolidated control of the town centre, seized the market place, hit the military police billets and took civilian hostages. As there had been no action in the town for some years and it was home to several senior South Vietnamese leaders, MACV was concerned that news of the assault would have a negative psychological effect across the country.

By 2 February it was clear that all the NVA regional units had been engaged across II Corps, but it had been noted that another division was waiting in reserve in the Central Highlands, west of Kontum and Pleiku. The situation in Kontum was particularly bad because, while one NVA battalion had fortified buildings, churches and pagodas across the town, the rest of the regiment was threatening to launch a new attack. Attacks against both Dak To and Kontum airfields stopped all but emergency flights landing and taking off, and it was only a matter of time before units ran short of ammunition. While Pleiku was quiet, there was a prolonged battle at Ta An to the south, where South Vietnamese irregulars fought off NVA attacks.

It was the same at Ban Me Thout where part of the 33rd NVA Regiment was occupying most of the town while the rest had the airfield under fire. The news from Da Lat was that the NVA and the ARVN were heavily engaged around the market place. On the coast, two convoys carrying South Koreans had been ambushed near Qui Nhon. Phan Thiet was also still under attack from three VC battalions, but when US troops helped the ARVN set up a blocking position, they were able to clear the town.

On 3 February, II Corps reported that it had been a quieter night and there were hopes that the NVA were withdrawing from the Central Highlands. While order was restored in Kontum, Pleiku and Ban Me Thout, early morning attacks in Dalat showed that the NVA had not given up. The Viet Cong, however, had withdrawn from most of the coastal towns; the last place to be cleared was Phan Thiet.

An M48 tank manned by ARVN troops forms a roadblock in downtown Saigon. (NARA-111-CCV-529)

By 4 February the fighting was over in II Corps. Widespread sweeps were being carried out around the main population centres as the police restored order on the streets and people returned home. Even so, Allied intelligence sources were keeping a close eye on the NVA forces, as they were regrouping in the Central Highlands. Would they attack again and, if so, when?

Attacks across III Corps

While there was plenty of action in the Central Highlands and in Saigon, III Corps, north and north-east of the capital, was the quietest area during the Tet Offensive, with the fewest attacks reported across the country. Even so, Xuan Loc, Phuoc Tuy, Hau Nghai and Tay Ninh were mortared and attacked on the first night of the offensive. Allied forces spent the next twenty-four hours deploying, counterattacking and restoring order. The only concerted attack on 2 February was made against the Cu Chi District headquarters; it failed. Instead, the Viet Cong resorted to mortaring 25th Division headquarters with 350 rounds, but the alarms made sure there were only a few casualties.

By 3 February the fighting across III Corps had been reduced to a handful of places, including Xuan Loc, Phuoc Le and Ba Rin. 1st Infantry Division's camps at Lai Khe and Quan Loi were also under rocket and mortar bombardment while 11th Armored Cavalry was engaged near Thu Duc, north-east of Saigon. On 4 February, III Corps reported the attacks were limited to Xuan Loc and Phouc Le bases, although 25th Infantry Division's camp at Cu Chi was again under mortar and rocket fire for the third time in a week. The attacks came to an end over the next twenty-four hours.

ARVN troops engage Viet Cong snipers in a narrow street. (NARA-111-CCV-529)

Attacks across IV Corps

South-west of Saigon, news from the towns across IV Corps was sporadic and confusing. While the VC Main Force units overran government and military targets in many provincial capitals, Local Force units had done the same in the district capitals. Fighting was reported in towns all across the Mekong Delta and there were concentrated attacks on military installations such as Soc Trang and Vinh Long airfields. The local ARVN units were finding it hard to restore order and requests for help from 9th ARVN Division were made as the fighting intensified.

The situation across the Mekong Delta remained confused and a lack of information usually meant that a town was still in enemy hands. While the general situation across IV Corps was improving, a fresh attack on Ben Tre, south-west of Saigon, caused heavy civilian casualties and further widespread collateral damage. By 2 February the Viet Cong were withdrawing from many towns and villages, having exhausted their ammunition, and the fighting was limited to a handful of provincial capitals such as Can Tho, Vinh Long, Ben Tre, Tien Giang and Moc Hoa. Elsewhere, only sporadic sniping and ambushes were being reported; but there were concerns that the Viet Cong were regrouping for a second wave of attacks.

The fighting was coming to an end across the Mekong Delta by 3 February, with enemy activity reduced to occasional sniper and mortar fire in most towns. On the whole, concerns about a second wave of attacks had failed to materialise in all but Ben Tre, where several hundred Viet Cong had infiltrated the town. While the ARVN were fighting hard to regain control of the towns across the Delta, it was taking longer than expected. The arrival of 9th Infantry Division's 2nd Brigade was expected to bring the fighting to a rapid close, but the damage had been done. The number of civilian casualties was growing daily and collateral damage was high, leaving thousands of people homeless. The longer it took to restore order, the harder it would be to restore the people's faith in the government.

PROLONGED BATTLES

The Battle for Hue Citadel

While the Marines were clearing the south bank of the Perfume River, 1st ARVN Division was fighting its own battle inside the Citadel walls. Three separate actions were developing and, while 1/3rd ARVN Regiment cleared the north-west corner, 1st ARVN Airborne Task Force was fighting from the centre towards the western wall and 4/2nd ARVN Regiment was fighting down the eastern wall toward the Imperial Palace.

Progress was slow and the fighting was hard, and General Truong had to readjust his lines across the Citadel on 5 February. While the three battalions of the Airborne task force secured the northern sector, 1/3rd ARVN Regiment recaptured the An Hoa gate at the north-west corner and 4/2nd ARVN Regiment advanced from the airfield to the south-west wall. Meanwhile, the rest of 3rd ARVN Regiment fought to clear the area between the south wall and the river.

During the early hours of 7 February, the NVA reinforcements used grappling hooks to climb the south-west wall. They took 4/2nd ARVN Regiment by surprise, forcing it back to the airstrip. When the clouds lifted later that morning, South Vietnamese planes swooped low over Hue, dropping bombs on the Citadel for the first time.

The NVA still controlled over half the Citadel and, so far, 1st Cavalry Division (Airmobile) had been unable to stop reinforcements entering it every night. General Truong decided to bring in his own reinforcements, using motorised junks to move three of 3rd ARVN Regiment's battalions to the northern gate. Once inside, they reinforced his compound and formed a base for counterattacks.

Meanwhile General Cushman needed to deploy more troops around Hue if he was going to seal off the city. When General Abrams opened MACV Forward Headquarters at Phu Bai on 12 February, he agreed to attach 101st Airborne Division's 1/327th Airborne Regiment to Task Force X-Ray.

While the battle for the Citadel was mainly an ARVN affair, on 9 February the 1/5th Marines were told they were going to join the battle inside its walls. The following morning Company A mounted a Rough Rider convoy in Phu Loc and rode to the Phu Lam Canal. After dismounting and crossing the broken An Cuu Bridge, the Marines walked through Hue's suburbs to the river. As the Marines entered the embattled city, 1st Battalion's howitzers were taking up positions around the city ready to give supporting fire. While the Emperors Palace of Perfect Peace and the Royal City were in a strict no-fire zone, 'Harassment and Interdiction' barrages could be fired at the wall surrounding the Palace grounds.

General Truong had ordered his own Marine Task Force to clear the east wall before the US Marines arrived. Although the heli-lift started on 11 February, bad weather put a stop to it and the ARVN Marine commander refused to let his men move by road; they had to wait two days for the mist to clear. Major Thong refused to commit his troops piecemeal and, by the time the US Marines arrived, the east wall was still in NVA hands.

On 11 February a Navy landing craft ferried Company A and five tanks along the Perfume River to General Truong's headquarters, while Company B was air-lifted in; Company C joined them the following day. As the three companies

THE CITADEL

The ARVN had a considerable number of men inside the Citadel, but there was never enough. General Truong had four airborne battalions, one infantry battalion, two armoured cavalry squadrons and the Black Panther Company. They were all finding it difficult to get the upper hand over the NVA in the tough urban battle.

assembled, they were told that an ARVN Airborne battalion was holding their deployment area and they would pass through their lines the following morning. But when Companies A and C advanced on the morning of 13 February, Major Robert H. Thompson reported how 'all hell broke loose. There was no Airborne unit in the area and Company A was up to their armpits in NVA.' His battalion suffered fifty-five casualties in a few minutes and Company B had to be relieved by Company A. Meanwhile, Company C advanced 300m towards an archway on the east wall. The large tower above the arch was the perfect firing position and the NVA was busy fortifying the area.

Thompson needed heavy support to crack the position but both the artillery and the Navy ships found it difficult to hit the tower. A break in the clouds the following morning allowed Marine F-4B Phantoms and F-8 Crusader jets to plaster the area with bombs and napalm. But the tower was still standing when the dust settled and the men inside were still up for a fight, stopping the Marines' next attack with heavy fire. Meanwhile, Major Thompson's Company D was still waiting to cross the Perfume River where the NVA had increased their presence along the riverbank. It was too dangerous for the Navy landing craft to cross and the Marines had to row across on junks.

Another round of shelling and bombing on the morning of 15 February brought part of the tower crashing to the ground. Company D renewed the attack and with the help of tanks, Ontos

'THE ALAMO'

Lieutenant Alexander W. Wells managed to sneak through the NVA lines and get into an ARVN-held Buddhist Temple. For the next two weeks he directed artillery and naval fire at targets across the Citadel. The temple was surrounded by NVA troops the whole time and Wells referred to his isolated position as 'The Alamo'.

Landing craft ferry Marines across the Perfume River to enter the battle in the Citadel. (NARA-Marine-190942)

and Company B, it reached the base of the tower after six hours of hard fighting. The final assault was led by Marine Private First Class John E. Holiday, who charged a bunker firing his machine-gun 'from the hip, John Wayne style'. The rest of Company D followed in an attack that cost six killed and over fifty wounded. Later that night the NVA crept back into the ruined tower and, by dawn, they were once again firing down on the Marines.

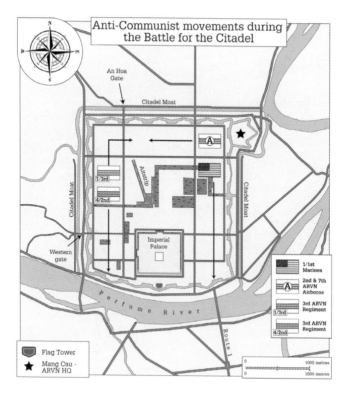

1/5th Marines joined the ARVN during the final battle for Hue Citadel.

1st Battalion advanced another 150m on 16 February but at a cost of fifty casualties. The Citadel had 'row after row of single-storey, thick-walled masonry houses jammed close together and occasionally separated by alleyways or narrow streets.' While the Marines were learning about street fighting, so were the NVA; they dug trenches, built roadblocks and fortified houses. It did not take much effort to build 'hundreds of naturally camouflaged, mutually supporting, fortified positions'.

Thompson's Marines felt like they were being fired at from all sides, and they were. Four- and five-storey houses stood beyond the eastern moat and NVA snipers could fire down

The six recoilless rifles of the Ontos were used to blast holes in walls and knock out NVA strongpoints. (NARA-Marine-370992)

over the Citadel wall at them. To the west 'the Imperial Palace provided the enemy a haven from which he could deliver small arms, rocket and mortar fire.' Major Thompson's Marines faced advancing through the killing ground between, and they had to wait because the landing craft bringing their ammunition and supplies was sunk in the Perfume River.

During the battle for Dong Ba tower, the Vietnamese Marine task force entered the battle for Hue and on 13 February landing craft ferried the 1st and 5th Marine Battalions across the Perfume River. They had to capture the south-west sector of the Citadel, starting by clearing the north side of the Imperial Palace before turning left along the west wall. The two battalions went into action on 14 February and, while 5th Battalion fought through the streets to reach its first objective, 1st Battalion took two days to capture a school. It took two days of hard fighting to advance just 400m.

While advances were being made in the southern half of the Citadel, the NVA counterattacked in the north, cutting off one battalion of 3rd ARVN Regiment; it took two days to reach it. However, the NVA did not have everything their own way. An enemy transmission ordering a battalion to attack through the west gate was intercepted on the night of 16 February. Marine 155mm howitzers and Navy gunships immediately fired, killing many, including the battalion commander. His successor was heard asking if he could withdraw and regroup; his request was denied.

Now that Marines were involved in the battle for the Citadel, US command was becoming increasingly concerned about any build-up of NVA forces. When General Abrams flew over 1st Cavalry's objective west of the city, there was still plenty of activity inside and outside the Citadel. The troops were supplied from a base camp 16km to the east and Abrams radioed General Cushman to warn him to expect a new offensive. They had to reinforce 3rd Brigade to increase pressure on the NVA forces building up north and west of Hue.

The same afternoon Generals Abrams, Cushman and Lahue met Vice President Nguyen Cao Ky and I Corps' Commander, Lieutenant General Hoang Xuan Lam, at Phu Bai. The Vice President agreed that US forces had to clear the NVA from the ancient pagodas and churches inside the Citadel and that he would accept responsibility for any damage suffered during the battle. General Westmoreland met Abrams and Cushman the following day and agreed to release more reinforcements to bring the battle to a conclusion as soon as possible.

The two battalions of 101st Airborne Division's 1st Brigade were added to Task Force X-Ray so they could block the area south and south-west of the city. Two more battalions were added to 1st Cavalry Division, 3rd Brigade, so they could seal off the north-west side of the city. It would allow 1/1st and 2/5th Marines to continue their operations east and south of Hue.

While the Allies reinforced the Hue area, the NVA was doing the same because they had kept their supply lines open. On 19 February two enemy battalions attacked the South Vietnamese Marines with the intention of opening an escape route for their senior officers and political leaders. It was a significant move because it meant they believed that the battle was lost.

Meanwhile, Major Thompson's Marines were stuck in front of a large, two-storey administrative building and he believed that 'if we could take this position, the rest would be easy.' But the advance had run out of steam and his men were exhausted.

On 20 February Abrams told Cushman: 'The measures so far taken are inadequate and not in consonance with the urgency of the problem or the resources you command. I direct that the resources owned by the US be unstintingly committed to the support of the Vietnamese forces of all types cutting out all the red tape and administrative procedures that in any way hinder the conduct of the battle.'

On the afternoon of the 20th, Major Thompson suggested making a night attack to take the building overlooking their position. Most of his company commanders were less than enthusiastic, but Lieutenant Patrick D. Polk's Company A was willing to give it a try. Staff Sergeant James Munroe and his three ten-man teams moved out at 3.00am on the 21st and found three key buildings, including the two-storey building, abandoned. A couple of hours later the NVA returned and were shot down before they could reoccupy the

MEDIA COVERAGE

The fierce fighting for the Citadel was happening in front of news correspondents and day after day American audiences were watching the battle unfold on their televisions. The news reports were undermining everyone's confidence in the ability of the US armed forces and one report by the Washington Post was a damning indictment of the Marines' ability to beat the NVA.

1/5th Marines fought a long, drawn-out battle in front of the press inside the Citadel walls. (NARA-Marine-A3-71377)

buildings. 1/5th Marines followed up the unexpected success, advancing to within 100m of the south-east wall. The following day Company A reached the wall and Lance Corporal James Avella hoisted a small American flag. It marked the beginning of the end for the NVA in the Citadel.

Company L, 3/5th Marines continued the advance to the southern gate, clearing the approaches to the road bridge across the Perfume River. Meanwhile, outside the walls, 1st Cavalry Division's 3rd Brigade assaulted the Que Chu area on 20 February; pushing the NVA back towards the Citadel over the next forty-eight hours.

While all was going well in the eastern half of the Citadel, the Vietnamese Marines were struggling to make progress to the west. It prompted Abrams to make a suggestion to Westmoreland on 23 February; he threatened to recommend the dissolution of the Vietnamese Marine Corps. The Marines

Marines carry their wounded comrade through the ruins of Hue. (NARA-Marine-A371947)

responded to the insult by renewing their attacks and cleared the south-west corner of the Citadel in record time. On the morning of the 24th a second Viet Cong flag was replaced, this time by one of the Republic of Vietnam.

After 3rd ARVN Regiment had secured the southern wall, the Black Panther Company joined the attack on the Imperial Palace; it soon fell because the NVA were looking to escape. One by one the final pockets of resistance inside the Citadel walls were silenced while ARVN Rangers cleared the area outside.

On 24 February, 1st Brigade, 101st Airborne Division and 2/5th Marines began its sweep south of the Perfume River, taking four days to clear the last groups of Viet Cong holding out south-west of the city. They then turned north-east to cut off the escape route to the coast and, on 2 March, the Marines declared Operation *Hue* complete. It had taken over four weeks to clear the city, four weeks during which the American people had seen their sons fighting for their lives in a gruelling battle.

The Siege of Khe Sanh Comes to an End

Between 30 January and 4 February the eyes of the world turned away from Khe Sanh to watch the Tet Offensive unfold across South Vietnam. But while Saigon, Hue, Da Nang and a host of other targets were attacked, 26th Marines did not let down their guard. It was only a matter of time before the NVA attacked Khe Sanh again.

On the nights of 4 and 5 February the sensors around Hill 881 South went crazy and it was estimated that around 2,000 soldiers

A mortar team returns fire at NVA targets outside the perimeter.
(NARA-Marine-374591)

were on the move. While artillery shelled the area, Captain Earle G. Breeding's Company E of the 2/26th Marines watched nervously from their trenches on Hill 861A. They had only just moved onto the hill and had nothing to build bunkers with.

At 5.00am on 5 February the hill came under heavy fire and, minutes later, around 200 North Vietnamese were spotted cutting their way through Company E's wire. While artillery shelled the hill, aircraft dropped napalm on the hill. But the NVA crept closer, forcing 1st Platoon to abandon its trenches. Lieutenant Don Shanley's platoon counterattacked, driving the NVA back and then shooting them down as they withdrew. The hill had been saved at the cost of seven dead and twenty-four wounded; around 100 enemy dead were later counted on the slopes.

The NVA's next target was Lang Vei Special Forces Camp on Route 9, 2km from the Laotian border. The heavily fortified position was held by Detachment A-101 of Company C, 5th Special Forces Group, and the four CIDG companies of Bru Montagnards they were training. 1km to the east was the village of Lang Vei, where the survivors of the Laotian Army Battalion attacked a few days earlier had gathered along with thousands of refugees. With so many NVA troops on the move in the area, the situation around Lang Vei was uncertain and dangerous.

At 12.30am on 7 February, twelve Soviet-built PT-76 light amphibious tanks of the 202nd Armour Regiment drove through the Lang Vei's camp fence and soldiers from 304th Division followed. It was one of the few times American troops faced tanks in the Vietnam War and they had little to stop them. Although the detachment's 106mm recoilless rifles knocked out a few of the tanks, it was only a matter of time before Detachment A-101 and the Bru Montagnards were overrun.

The survivors took cover inside their bunkers while the tanks parked on top and NVA soldiers tossed fragmentation and gas grenades inside. Captain Frank Willoughby resorted to calling in air and artillery support on top of his own position, despite the dangers to his own men. A new type of controlled

AMPHIBIOUS TANKS

The Soviet-built PT-76 tank was armed with a 76.2mm main gun and a coaxial medium machine-gun. It was designed to be deployed on reconnaissance missions and the boat-shaped hull allowed it to cross water with the help of two hydro jets, two bilge pumps and a trim vane.

fragmentation ammunition, codenamed 'Firecracker', was used for the first time and, while it devastated the NVA, they still kept coming.

Willoughby requested support from Khe Sanh, but Colonel Lownds refused because the airstrip was under continuous fire and ground sensors indicated another attack was imminent. To send troops out on to Route 9 at night with enemy tanks on the prowl was considered suicidal. Generals Westmoreland, Cushman and Tompkins all had to accept Lownds' decision; Willoughby's men were on their own.

On the morning of 7 February General Westmoreland met Cushman and other senior commanders at Da Nang. Colonel Jonathan E. Ladd, commander of 5th Special Forces Group, wanted either to relieve or evacuate Lang Vei Camp; Lieutenant Colonel Daniel L. Baldwin III, the northern Studies and Observations Group commander (in charge of covert missions) agreed.

General Westmoreland consented to provide helicopter and fixed-wing support, but while it was being organised Willoughby's Special Forces team and the Montagnards broke out of the camp and headed for Lang Vei village. There they tried in vain to get the Laotians to help them, but pandemonium broke out. The crowds mobbed the Marine helicopters when they landed. Events on Lang Vei had happened too quickly. 300 of the camp's 487 defenders were killed, wounded, or missing. Of Willoughby's twenty-four-strong unit, ten were dead or missing while another thirteen had been wounded.

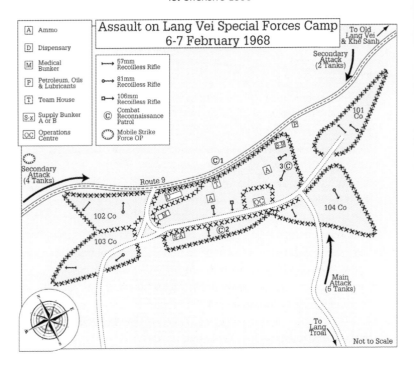

The 6,000 Laotians and Vietnamese left behind by the helicopters walked to Khe Sanh base, only for Lownds to refuse them entry; he was worried there were NVA infiltrators in the crowd. Instead the gate guards were ordered to use CS gas or fire over their heads to disperse them; they would have to shoot into the crowds if the security of the base was compromised.

During the early hours of 8 February elements of 101D NVA Regiment crept through thick fog towards 1/9th Marines outpost, Alpha 1. The sappers threw canvas over the barbed wire, rolled over it and entered the perimeter, taking the Marines by surprise. In the hand-to-hand battle that followed, over a dozen of Lieutenant Terence R. Roach's men were killed but the rest fought back. At dawn, a second platoon went to the rescue, shooting down over 150 NVA as they tried to escape.

Roach's garrison had suffered fifty-one casualties out of sixty-six and Colonel Lownds gave instructions to abandon the outpost; it was too dangerous to hold on to.

Between 5 and 8 February the NVA had made three assaults against targets around Khe Sanh base, but the only success had been at Lang Vei. From now on they would focus all their attentions on the base itself. Night after night, hundreds of metres of shallow trenches were dug, some starting over a kilometre from the base and ending just outside the barbed wire. It was disturbing to watch the NVA burrow closer, but there was little the Marines could do to stop them. While shells, bombs, rockets and napalm showered the area around the perimeter, the NVA kept digging.

It also appeared that new anti-aircraft guns were being dragged onto the hills surrounding the airstrip, forcing the cargo planes to run a gauntlet of fire every time they landed and took off. On 10 February a KC-130 was shot down in front of a camera crew and the footage was soon being watched on television sets across the US. The intensity of enemy shelling increased during the last week of February, rising to a crescendo on the 23rd when over 1,300 rounds hit the base. One shell hit Ammunition Supply Point Number 3, detonating 1,600 rounds of 90mm and 106mm ammunition. And still the NVA dug closer.

On 25 February a platoon-sized patrol from Company B, 1/26th Marines, was ambushed while investigating trenches in front of its perimeter. A second platoon was sent out to help, but it too came under heavy fire. Between them the two platoons suffered nearly fifty casualties and half of them were missing in action. During the gun battle it became clear that the NVA were building camouflaged bunkers close to the base perimeter and Colonel Lownds restricted future patrolling to prevent further disasters.

The NVA chose to make their move during the early hours of 29 February and sappers prepared the perimeter in front of 37th ARVN Ranger Battalion, cutting wire, removing mines and disabling trip flares. Their work was discovered the following

NVA SHELLING

The NVA guns kept shelling Khe Sanh base and the bombardment increased in intensity when bad weather stopped air observers flying overhead. 3rd Marine Division commander, General Tompkins, commented that the area looked like 'pictures of the surface of the moon, in that it was cratered and pocked and blasted.'

A damaged KC-130 sits stranded on the Khe Sanh airstrip. (NARA-Marine-191092)

morning and the Rangers were placed on full alert. The following night 304th Division's 66th Regiment crept forward through thick fog, tracked all the way by electronic sensors. Artillery shelled the leading battalion just outside the perimeter, while two B-52 airstrikes decimated the reserve battalion. The attack never materialised and the survivors melted away.

It appears that the NVA knew the ARVN Rangers were holding the eastern end of the base and considered them to be

'Welcome to Khe Sanh' – the sign waiting for new arrivals on the airstrip control tower. (NARA-Marine-1889984)

a weak link in the perimeter. They concentrated their attacks against them for the remainder of the siege, making another seven attacks during March, including a large scale assault on the 18th.

As February drew to a close, the weather conditions eased as the monsoon season came to an end. It meant that air supply was more reliable; but as the air above Khe Sanh became busier, so did the volume of anti-aircraft fire. Several C-123 cargo planes, CH-46 and UH-1 helicopters were damaged or destroyed running the gauntlet of fire on the flight path.

After eight long weeks and no breakthrough, the North Vietnamese propaganda teams moved through the Montagnard villages in the Central Highlands with a new message: 'Ho Chi Minh would be unhappy if they [the NVA] wasted their time on only 6,000 Marines at Khe Sanh!' It was a way of saying that troops were going to withdraw to focus on the bigger picture.

At the same time Allied intelligence noted withdrawals on the ground as 525C Division crossed the border into Laos, 304th Division withdrew to the south-west. Even so, the NVA artillery continued to do their worst and when over 1,000 rounds hit the base on 22 March, Ammunition Supply Point 1 was hit again; this time 4,000 rounds detonated.

By the end of March Colonel Lownds felt it was time for 26th Marines to strike back, and 1st Battalion made the first attack against Hill 421 on the 31st. While artillery strikes hit the area around an NVA position with a box of fire, promised air support was cancelled due to low cloud cover. Company B advanced onto the hill and, while they destroyed one bunker complex, they could not locate the remains of the men lost over a month before. By the time Company B was back inside the wire it had suffered 112 casualties.

The siege of Khe Sanh was designated an extension of Operation *Scotland*, the operation to reinforce and hold the combat base. It had started on 1 November 1967 and came to an end on 31 March 1968 after five long, hard months.

OPERATION *SCOTLAND*

The logistics of Operation *Scotland* were staggering. 24,449 sorties had been flown over the Khe Sanh area and 103,500 tons of ordnance had been dropped on the NVA positions. The two battalions of artillery based in the area had fired over 102,000 rounds. The North Vietnamese had replied with nearly 11,000 rounds, every one of them carried by hand onto the hills surrounding Khe Sanh.

Allied casualties were 205 killed in action and 1,668 wounded; around half of them evacuated from the battlefield. While the official NVA casualty count was 1,602 dead and only seven prisoners, the intelligence estimates were far less conservative; they ranged from 10,000 to 15,000 casualties.

Route 9 connected Khe Sanh with civilisation but it had been impassable for some time owing to continual mining and numerous damaged bridges. A heavy NVA presence made sure that the Allies had to make a concerted effort to reopen it. When intelligence reports recorded that the NVA were moving missiles into the DMZ and northern Quang Tri Province, the time had come to reopen Route 9 and regain the initiative in the area. General Cushman and General Abrams approved the plan on 2 March and, eight days later, General Westmoreland agreed. The operation would be codenamed *Pegasus* and the objective was to open Route 9 as far as Khe Sanh.

Lieutenant General William B. Rosson was the commander of the new Provisional Corps that had taken control of the northern sector of I Corps and he had 1st Cavalry Division, 101st Airborne Division and 3rd Marine Division under his control. He assigned the mission to Major General John J. Tolson, commander of the 1st Cavalry Division, who began detailed planning with the 3rd Marine Division.

The plan was for the Air Cavalry to leapfrog the damaged culverts and bridges, and then clear an area around a section

127

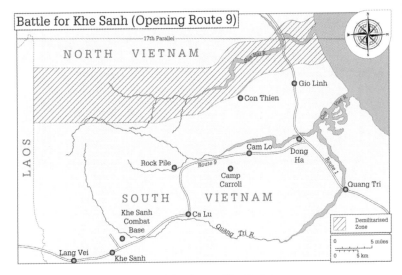

Route 9 had to be opened to end the siege of Khe Sanh base.

of road. Once a perimeter had been secured, the engineers would move up to remove the mines and bridge the streams. As soon as the road was open for wheeled traffic, the Air Cavalry would leapfrog ahead again. 1st Marine Regiment, the 11th Engineers, and a Construction Battalion (known as the Seabees) were added to Tolson's command, while an ARVN airborne task force of three battalions was also promised. It increased the task force to over 30,000 troops, making Operation *Pegasus* the largest offensive in the area south of the DMZ to date.

The operation began with the building of a new base for the 1st Cavalry Division at Ca Lu, 16km east of Khe Sanh. A landing strip large enough for Fairchild C-123 Provider cargo aircraft was built, along with supply and medical facilities, and the base was called Landing Zone Stud.

On 26 March 1st Squadron, 9th Cavalry began helicopter reconnaissance patrols, looking for suitable landing zones along Route 9. While observation helicopters directed airstrikes, the planes used delay-fused 'daisy cutter' bombs to create landing zones for the Air Cavalry. On 30 March, 3rd Marine Division began two days of diversionary attacks north-east of Dong Ha when Task Force Kilo advanced along the coastal plains near Gio Linh.

On the morning of 1 April bad weather grounded all helicopters, so it was left to the 1st Marines to advance along Route 9 while 11th Engineer Battalion followed, removing mines, clearing obstacles and repairing crossings. When the weather cleared in the afternoon, 3rd Brigade was airlifted and by nightfall it had secured landing zones west of the 1st Marines. Poor early morning weather and the lack of enemy contact dictated the pattern of operations for the next three days.

A 1st Cavalry Division air assault; artillery targetted the hills, while helicopters delivered men to the landing zone. (NARA-111-CCV-97)

On 4 April 1/9th Marines advanced from the perimeter of Khe Sanh base and helped the Air Cavalry take Hill 471; it was the first time the Marines had left their trenches in force for seventy-five days. Early the following morning, attacks by the 66th NVA Regiment were dispersed by artillery fire. Other units of the Khe Sanh garrison also went on the offensive, probing the area around the base for the first time since the siege began.

On 6 April, 26th Marines started patrolling the area outside its perimeter. 2nd Battalion ran into an ambush near Hill 558 and it took all day for them to withdraw to safety, taking their fifty casualties with them. The following day it cleared the ridge while 1st Battalion probed the area to the south, recovering the bodies lost by Company B many weeks earlier.

To the east, 1st Marines continued to advance slowly towards Khe Sanh while 1st Cavalry Division's 3rd Brigade made another air assault, which resulted in a tough battle with the NVA. At midday on 6 April first contact was made between the Air Cavalry and the Marines when 2/12th Cavalry landed on Hill 471, allowing 1/9th Marines to advance onto Hills 689 and Hill 552. The following day 1st Air Cavalry Division's 2nd Brigade captured an old French fort near Khe Sanh Village while 3rd Brigade and the 1st Marines moved along Route 9 ahead of the engineers, finding no NVA in the area.

At 8.00am on 8 April, 2/7th Cavalry entered Khe Sanh combat base, bringing the seventy-nine-day siege to an end. As the Air Cavalry's 3d Brigade moved into the perimeter, the 26th Marines prepared to depart. The following day the airstrip opened and on 11 April Route 9 was open to traffic. The Seabees had repaired 14km of road, rebuilt nine bridges and bypassed seventeen other damaged crossings.

While 1st Cavalry Division began to withdraw to Camp Evans, the 1st and 26th Marines continued offensive operations around Khe Sanh and, on 14 April, the Stars and Stripes were raised on Hill 881 North. On 15 April 3rd Marine Division once again assumed responsibility for Khe Sanh combat base and as Operation *Pegasus* came to a close, Operation *Scotland* resumed.

AFTER THE BATTLE

The Military Outcome

What could the Allies have done differently to reduce the impact of the Tet Offensive? While MACV intelligence knew that a countrywide offensive was imminent, General Westmoreland was overly attentive to the NVA's build up around Khe Sanh, near the DMZ. MACV noted the movement of known Viet Cong members in and around towns and cities across the rest of the country, but they believed the majority were visiting their families for the Tet festivities.

While no one was ready for the scale or ferocity of the attacks across South Vietnam, MACV prudently cancelled the holiday ceasefire, stopped all leave and placed military installations on alert. It also correctly noted that the premature attack around Da Nang on 30 January was a foretaste of what was to come twenty-four hours later.

When the attacks began, many were stopped in their tracks, particularly those made against military installations. Where the Viet Cong and NVA managed to breach perimeters, order was generally restored in a few hours, while casualties were minimal. However, it was a different story in urban areas where the attacks were much harder to contain. Naturally, it took time to assess the enemy dispositions and objectives, and it then took more time to deploy reinforcements and restore order. But once the American and South Vietnamese forces arrived, they usually dealt with the NVA and Viet Cong incursions quickly. Or at least they dealt with organised resistance quickly. Small groups and individuals continued to fight on for days and, in some cases, as in the Cholon district of Saigon, weeks. To many it appeared that the government was struggling to deal with the Communist threat.

One major headache for the Allies was Hue Citadel, where the ARVN were left to their own devices for some time. While the

The constant stream of combat footage on television undermined the American public's confidence in the war and in their military commanders. (NARA-Marine-A371355)

Marines took only ten days to secure the suburbs south of the Perfume River, it took over four weeks to secure the Citadel to the north. It was four weeks of relentless urban combat, where some of most gruelling fighting in the Vietnam War was reported and shown on American television.

In Khe Sanh, all the Marines could do was to wait for the NVA siege to run out of steam. As long as supplies could be flown in, they could hold out. For seventy-nine days the Marines sat tight, fending off the enemy probes in a battle of attrition that was stacked against the NVA. Again, news reporters photographed and filmed the combat, the explosions, the burning planes and helicopters, and the casualties. All across the United States, Americans watched as their soldiers fought for their lives; their sons, brothers and cousins.

Although the generals and the politicians had repeatedly insisted the war was being won, the news reports made it look as if they had been dishonest, changing the mood of the nation. While the Tet Offensive had been a serious military defeat for the NVA and the Viet Cong, it had been a serious political defeat for the United States.

The Mini-Tet Offensive, May 1968

By the end of April, Communist units were preparing for the second phase of the Tet Offensive, which would become known as the 'Mini-Tet' or the 'Little Tet'. Yet again, Allied intelligence predicted the attacks and both military bases and government buildings across the country were on full alert. Early on 5 May 1968, NVA and Viet Cong units attacked 119 targets across South Vietnam. This time most were stopped by the US and ARVN troops before they could infiltrate the perimeters and cause havoc.

Thousands of NVA and Viet Cong soldiers had infiltrated Saigon once more, and no less than thirteen battalions attacked targets across the capital. It took two days of heavy fighting to clear 267th Local Force Battalion out of the Phu Lam district in

ARVN paratroopers engage a Viet Cong position with grenades and M60 machine-guns while their comrades move closer. (NARA-111-CCV-317)

western Saigon. Other targets were Tan Son Nhut airfield to the north and Y-Bridge to the south. By 12 May the attacks were over and the NVA and Viet Cong forces withdrew from the city, leaving behind over 3,000 dead.

As the fighting around Saigon died down, the military and the press became focused on a new attack against Kham Duc Special Forces Camp, in Quang Tin Province, in the north of the country. US intelligence had been tracking 2nd NVA Division since the end of March, watching as it moved down the Ho Chi Minh Trail and across the border into South Vietnam, heading straight for the camp. While Kham Duc's base defences were being improved and the runway was extended, 11th Mobile Strike Force (known as Mike Force) established a second base at Ngok Tavak, an old French fort 8km south of Kham Duc. The Chinese Nung force and their three Australian advisors were supposed to locate, track and report enemy movements, but instead it was the 1st Viet Cong Regiment who watched them dig in.

Kham Duc and Ngok Tavak stood right in 2nd NVA Division's path and early on 10 May two of its regiments made their move. Kham Duc was shelled and, although 11th Mike Force reinforced Ngok Tavak, it had to be evacuated on 11 May. 1st Viet Cong Regiment then turned its attention to Kham Duc, where 1,800 US and South Vietnamese troops were soon under siege. While the Americal Division airlifted reinforcements, in what was called Operation *Golden Valley*, the outposts fell one by one as the noose tightened around the base.

Westmoreland wanted to avoid another Khe Sanh-style siege and, at midday on 12 May, MACV gave the order to extract all personnel. 834th Air Division immediately began to evacuate the camp, losing nine aircraft, including two C-130 transport aircraft, to heavy enemy fire over the hours that followed. The evacuation was disorderly and, at times, panicky, and abandoning the base was a major defeat for the US military.

The NVA and Viet Cong launched more attacks in Saigon on 25 May, only this time they ignored military installations and seized six pagodas in the belief that they would give protection from artillery and air attacks. They did not, but the sight of these religious structures being pounded by shells was bad propaganda for the Allies. Once again, most of the fighting occurred in the predominantly Chinese suburb of Cholon, where it dragged on for over three weeks. The only highlight of the fighting for the Allies was the surrender of over 150 soldiers of the Quyet Thang Regiment to ARVN forces on 18 June; it was the largest number of prisoners taken together during the war.

While the Allies were able to claim a military triumph, casualties had again been high, while collateral damage was extensive. Between 5 and 30 May, 1,161 US soldiers and airmen were killed and another 3,954 were wounded, far greater than the numbers suffered during the opening attacks of the January Tet Offensive. Over 500 civilians were killed and 4,500 were wounded; 87,000 were made homeless. Yet again the NVA and Viet Cong had wreaked death and destruction on the people of Saigon.

The War Continues

Battalion-size operations continued over the summer of 1968 as US and Allied forces tracked down the scattered Viet Cong and North Vietnamese forces. Operation *Pegasus* relieved Khe Sanh combat base on 5 April, while Operation *Delaware* soon regained control of the A Shau Valley, forcing the NVA to call off attacks across I Corps. The emphasis moved to III Corps on 5 May, when the Viet Cong attacked Saigon; but the NVA and the Viet Cong soon withdrew to their sanctuaries. The NVA's final offensive on 17 August was quickly brought under control and stopped.

US troops then turned their attentions to supporting the South Vietnamese government pacification program, clearing populated areas so ARVN troops could take control. Regional Force and Popular Force then took over responsibility for security, while the police screened anyone on the move, looking to arrest Viet Cong sympathisers. The Accelerated Pacification Campaign was extended into the countryside while military operations along the border forced Viet Cong units out of South Vietnam and into Laos and Cambodia.

In October 1968 President Johnson announced that the bombing of North Vietnam would end while the National Liberation Front and South Vietnam were invited to join peace talks in Paris for the first time. Richard Nixon was elected president in November 1968 and, two months later, he announced that the first US combat troops would be withdrawn at the same time as peace negotiations opened in Paris.

On 23 February 1969 attacks were made against military installations across I Corps in a new offensive; they were all stopped in their tracks. Over seventy ground operations followed, but the Viet Cong and NVA managed to avoid contact every time. While American troop strength had peaked at 543,400 in April 1968, the number had fallen to 505,500 by October and President Nixon announced more troop withdrawals as ground operations were wound down.

Vietnamisation programs now became the norm as US troops taught the South Vietnamese Armed Forces how to fight effectively, preparing them to take over military operations. By the spring of 1970 the situation was under control in South Vietnam and attention turned to the Communist bases across the border in Cambodia. As the NVA and Viet Cong threatened to overthrow Cambodia's capital, Phnom Penh, Prime Minister Lon Nol appealed for help. President Nixon responded immediately and US and ARVN troops crossed the border at eight points in May and June. While Operation *Rock Crusher* discovered well developed base areas and captured huge quantities of material, it could only delay the NVA's plans, not stop them.

On 30 January 1971 attention turned north when South Vietnamese troops crossed into Laos and attacked the Ho Chi Minh Trail around Techepone. After a promising start they fell back across the border in disarray. While Operation *Lam Son 719* had failed to achieve its objectives, it had interrupted the North Vietnamese Army's plans for a March offensive.

On 11 July 1971 the ARVN assumed full control of ground operations while the final US military operation ended in October. In August President Nixon announced that Phase I of Vietnamisation was coming to an end and the remaining 191,000 US troops in South Vietnam would only be used to protect bases and support South Vietnamese units; they would not carry out any more offensive operations. By the end of the year Phase II ended, leaving only 25,000 US troops behind to protect military installations. Meanwhile, air attacks on North Vietnam increased in the hope of disrupting future NVA offensives against South Vietnam and Cambodia.

Although peace proposals were exchanged during this period, little headway was made towards ending the war in South Vietnam. While Nixon proposed withdrawing all troops within six months of an agreement being made, the Communists wanted them all to leave and aid to stop before they would agree to a ceasefire.

As long as the fighting continued, the people of South Vietnam suffered. (NARA-111-CCV-377)

The NVA launched an offensive on 30 March 1972, aiming to capture large areas of the country. The ARVN counterattacked in September with the help of US Army helicopters and planes. But time was running out as American advisors gave their final lessons to the South Vietnamese Air Force pilots and the last seven battalions handed over responsibility for their military installations and headed home. Only support and service units remained behind to help the South Vietnamese.

THE LEGACY

Reaction to the Tet Offensive

While it only took a few days to restore order across South Vietnam, the repercussions of the Tet Offensive would be felt for much longer, both in Southeast Asia and the United States.

If there was one area where the Viet Cong failed, it was in raising civilian support for their cause. While the people were impressed with the scale of the offensive, they were outraged that their sacred Tet celebrations had been violated. Many had heard of Communist atrocities, but they had always been in the far-flung provinces. Now for the first time the people in the towns and cities saw, or suffered from, the violence and mayhem caused by the NVA and Viet Cong. Death, injury and destruction affected almost every family directly or indirectly. For the majority, the Tet Offensive meant that the Viet Cong could not be trusted and the threat of a Viet Cong takeover brought the people together for a while.

While the majority of people blamed the government for failing to prepare against the attacks, they did support its response to the attacks. The swift action by ARVN troops and the resumption of control by the National Police restored the people's faith in the Saigon administration. There was also a favourable reaction to the US role in dealing with the NVA and the Viet Cong. However, a

America's youth was being used to fight an unpopular war which was being seen as unwinnable. (NARA-Marine-A185146)

surprisingly large number of people believed that the US had connived with the Viet Cong to undermine the government. Why would they think such a thing? It was because they were convinced that things only happened in South Vietnam if the Americans made them happen.

The reaction to the Tet Offensive on the other side of the Pacific was very different. US troops had been in South Vietnam for nearly three years by February 1968 and General Westmoreland had consistently reported positively about progress against the Viet Cong. Campaigns were reported as successful, hamlets were being returned to government control, body counts were high and weapons caches were numerous. It was exactly what the politicians and the press wanted to hear.

The Vietnam War was a war with no frontlines and new indicators had to be found to replace the traditional results relating to ground captured and distances advanced. While statistics had to be analysed relating to tangible military targets, they also had to be related to vague social and political targets such as improvements in education, medicine, trade and public opinion. While Westmoreland and his staff kept reporting successes, the Viet Cong were stockpiling weapons and ammunition ready to attack targets across South Vietnam. Meanwhile, the NVA were moving troops down the Ho Chi Minh Trail in Laos, ready to cross the border.

By the end of 1967 both Washington and Saigon were looking to end the conflict because war weariness was increasing. As casualties mounted it was becoming harder to justify, particularly to the people of America who were tired of the constant stream of war reports from Southeast Asia.

By the end of 1967 President Lyndon B. Johnson's term was in its final year and Richard Nixon announced he intended to run in the New Year election. The primary election season began just as the Tet Offensive was launched and when Johnson withdrew from the campaign after a poor result in the New Hampshire primary, it was seen by many as a rejection of the Democrats' policies in

South Vietnam. The election season then had another shock when Senator Robert F. Kennedy was assassinated shortly after winning the Californian primary.

Nixon often appeared on television during the election campaign making comments and promises about the war in Southeast Asia. He stated that 'a new leadership will end the war and win the peace in the Pacific.' He would negotiate 'peace with honour'. He also promised to bring an end to civil unrest across America, much of it associated with the anti-war movement and those who opposed their position.

The public, press and political reactions to the Tet Offensive had an impact on the 1968 election, increasing the Republican share of the vote to a point where Nixon beat Hubert Humphrey by nearly half a million votes at the end of the year. He was inaugurated as the 37th President of the United States on 20 January 1969.

The Withdrawal of Combat Troops

Richard Nixon's administration immediately began planning how to withdraw ground troops from South Vietnam. Vietnamisation programs, designed to hand over responsibility to South Vietnam's armed forces, were announced in March. In June Nixon announced that the first withdrawal of 25,000 troops would begin the following month; it was the start of a three-year process.

The withdrawals caused many problems in the field as troops became frustrated, bored and resentful while they waited for their twelve month tour to end. Most now believed the war was a lost cause and by 1971 morale started to disintgrate as crime, racially motivated incidents, drug abuse and disobedience increased. Once back in the US, many veterans had no interest in completing the rest of their service and their discontentment spread to new recruits.

News reports during these troubled times created a feeling of mistrust between Vietnam veterans and those of the Second World War and Korea for years to come. Few became involved

A helicopter is pushed off the deck of an aircraft carrier to make way for others waiting to land. (NARA-Navy-K-108267)

in the Veterans of Foreign Wars or the American Legion. Only in recent years have veterans begun to say they were proud of their service in Vietnam. Many prefer the company of other veterans, particularly from their own unit, and as they approach retirement age many take the time to look back on the defining years in their lives and remember their fallen comrades with pride.

The NVA's Final Offensive

On 10 March 1975 the NVA launched a new offensive in South Vietnam, capturing Ban Me Thuot and one of the main roads through the Central Highlands. President Nguyen Van Thieu ordered his forces to withdraw from the mountains around Kontum and Pleiku, but rather than regrouping, the ARVN fell back in disorder while panicked air crews evacuated their families. The NVA attack resumed on the 16th and the ARVN fell back to Qui Nhon, abandoning over sixty aircraft. As the NVA increased attacks across I Corps, tens of thousands (including many soldiers) headed to the coast where they were evacuated by American ships. Chaos reigned as Phu Cat airbase and 180 planes fell into enemy hands.

At the same time, the Khmer Rouge, the followers of the Cambodian Communist Party, seized the country's capital, Phnom Penh. On 12 April Operation *Eagle Pull* was launched and Marines established a perimeter around Landing Zone Hotel near the American Embassy. An hour later 276 people, including eighty-two Americans, were on helicopters and on their way to US Navy carriers in the Gulf of Thailand. Cambodia fell to the Communists five days later.

Meanwhile, in South Vietnam, the Vietnamese Air Force abandoned Nha Trang and Cam Ranh Bay airbases as the exodus continued, with many people being taken by ship to the Gulf of Siam. Thirteen NVA divisions began closing in on Saigon and when Xuan Loc, Bien Hoa and Tan Son Nhut bases were abandoned on 23 April, there was nowhere for planes and helicopters to land.

While US Navy helicopters evacuated American personnel and Vietnamese officials, Vietnamese pilots flew their families to Thailand or one of the US aircraft carriers. Many helicopters had to be pushed overboard or crashed into the sea. On 29 April, President Gerald Ford ordered the evacuation of personnel from Saigon, codename Operation *Frequent Wind*. 850 Marines secured a landing zone while helicopters evacuated nearly 400 US citizens and 4,500 Vietnamese officials and their families. As Operation *Frequent Wind* came to an end, the Marine commander learnt that several hundred Americans and thousands more Vietnamese were trapped at the US Embassy in the heart of the city. He had to organise a new airlift from the embassy's walled compound.

Helicopters landed in the small compound or on the tiny rooftop helipad as thousands gathered around the Embassy, looking to escape. Although the evacuation continued throughout the night, the crowds increased until Washington ordered the helicopters to evacuate the American staff only, leaving their Vietnamese comrades behind. At 5.00am on 30 April, Ambassador Martin stepped onboard a helicopter and, three hours later, the last Marine left. While 2,000 had been rescued, hundreds of

Vietnamese were left behind at the Embassy and thousands of government employees had to be left to their fate across Saigon.

The same day NVA troops moved into the capital and the remaining South Vietnamese forces surrendered. The struggle for South Vietnam was over, a little more than ten years after the Marines first landed at Da Nang.

The Human Cost

Around 2.6 million American men and women served in South Vietnam and around half experienced combat or served in close support. They were divided between the services as follows:

Army, 1,736,000   Air Force, 293,000
Marine Corps, 391,000   Navy, 174,000

While the first US casualty occurred in 1957, 97 per cent of the men lost their lives between 1965 and 1973. The bloodiest fighting occurred in 1968, the year of the Tet Offensive, when there were 16,589 casualties, divided between the services as follows:

Army 38,196   Air Force, 2,583
Marine Corps, 14,837   Navy, 2,555

One sobering fact is that approximately 11,500 of the men who died were 20 years old or younger. Over 303,000 men were wounded, 75,000 of them were severely disabled.

During the first week of the Tet Offensive, the NVA and Viet Cong suffered over 32,000 killed, while another 5,800 were captured. US losses for the same period were over 1,000 and over 2,800 ARVN were killed. South Vietnamese losses were much higher because the NVA and Viet Cong attacked bases held by ARVN troops, believing them to be 'softer' targets.

Most of the fighting was in urban areas and, while over 7,000 civilians were killed, thousands more were injured. Tens of thousands

The rising number of casualties was the price to be paid for being involved in Southeast Asia. (NARA-Marine-A184379)

were forced to flee to escape the fighting and many returned to find their homes in ruins. It is estimated that 5,000 were executed by Viet Cong cadres, many of them in Hue where several mass graves were discovered. The majority were police and army officers, government officials, teachers, doctors, and political leaders.

Remembering

11 November has been the day when America remembers its war dead since 1919, the first anniversary of the Armistice marking the end of the First World War. At 11.00am two minutes silence is respected in ceremonies across the country, with the national ceremony held in Arlington Cemetery, Virginia. Congress made the day a national holiday in 1938 and the town of Emporia, Kansas, first used the name Veteran's Day in 1953. Congress adopted the name in time for the 1954 Veteran's Day.

Veterans set up a Memorial Fund in 1979 to raise funds for a memorial to those who lost their lives in the Vietnam War and a site in Constitution Gardens, close to the Lincoln Memorial, was

'The Wall' – America's memorial to those who fought and died in
Vietnam. (Author's collection)

donated in 1980. Following a national competition, Maya Ying
Lin's design for a memorial wall, with two partially sunken walls
laid out in a large V-shape, was accepted. The memorial was
dedicated in November 1982 and visitors were able to search for
the name of their loved ones or comrades on the black polished
granite walls. In 2006 there were 58,253 names on 'The Wall'.

The Stars and Stripes always flies on a nearby flagpole and
on memorial days it is joined by the Missing in Action flag. A
traditional bronze sculpture and a memorial remembering the
7,500 women who had served in the war complete the area.

Remembering those still 'Missing in Action'. (Author's collection)

2,583 servicemen were still missing at the end of the war, but countless searches located many unmarked graves and the remains were returned to the United States. By 2007 the number was down to 1,788. The flag of the National League of Families of American Prisoners and Missing in South East Asia has a black background and a white silhouetted head, bowed below a guard tower. The words 'You are not forgotten' are at the bottom. The people of America will make sure they never are.

ORDERS OF BATTLE

US Armed Forces Order of Battle

Virtually every unit in the Marine Corps, Army and Air Force was affected by the Tet Offensive. What follows are the main Marine Corps and Army units involved in engaging the NVA and Viet Cong.

I Corps

1st Marine Division
  1st and 5th Marine Regiments engaged in Hue
  7th and 27th Marine Regiments engaged in Da Nang
  26th Marine Regiment, siege of Khe Sanh
3rd Marine Division stationed along the Demilitarized Zone
23rd Infantry Division (Americal) stationed south of Da Nang
101st Airborne Division (Screaming Eagles) engaged at Hue and Phu Bai

II Corps

1st Cavalry Division (Airmobile) based at An Khe in the Central Highlands
4th Infantry Division based at Pleiku in the Central Highlands
173d Airborne Brigade stationed at An Khe in the Central Highlands

III Corps
1st Infantry Division stationed north of Saigon
25th Infantry Division stationed at Cu Chi, north-west of Saigon
199th (Light) Infantry Brigade engaged in Saigon
11th Armored Cavalry Regiment engaged in Saigon and Long Binh

IV Corps
9th Infantry Division south of Saigon and in the Mekong Delta
Across the Country
5th Special Forces Group (Airborne) fire bases along the western border
Reinforcements
3rd Brigade, 82nd Airborne Division, was airlifted from the United States to Chu Lai by 140 planes.
It landed on 18 February and joining 101st Airborne Division as it battled for Hue.

South Vietnamese Army (ARVN) Order of Battle

I Corps; Marine Corps (two brigades);
1st, 2nd and 3rd Infantry Divisions
II Corps; 22nd and 23rd Division
III Corps; Airborne Division; 5th, 18th and 25th Infantry Divisions
IV Corps; 7th, 9th and 21st Infantry Divisions
Deployed Across the Country
Ranger Battalions
Regional Forces (150,000 militia) and Popular Forces (150,000 militia)
Civilian Irregular Defence Groups (42,000 militia)

NVA and Viet Cong Order of Battle

It is estimated 84,000 regular and irregular troops attacked during the opening stages of the Tet Offensive. MACV reported the following number of confirmed battalions in January 1968:

I Corps: 16 VC and 53 NVA battalions
II Corps: 15 VC and 35 NVA battalions
III Corps: 39 VC and 20 NVA battalions
IV Corps: 29 VC battalions

The NVA was controlled by Military Regions and while MRs 1 to 4 covered North Vietnam, MRs 5 to 9 covered South Vietnam:

Military Region 5 from the DMZ south to Ban Ma Thuot and Cam Ranh

Military Region 6 the coastal area south from Cam Ranh

Military Region 7 covered the area north-west and north-east of Saigon

Military Region 8 covered the area south and west of Saigon

Military Region 9 covered the Mekong Delta

Military Region 10 was to the west of Military Regions 6 and 7

The Viet Cong was controlled by five B Fronts;

B1 Front covered the coastal region from Da Nang down to Cam Ranh

B2 Front south of Ban Ma Thuot and Cam Ranh including Saigon and the Mekong Delta

B3 Front covered the Central Highlands as far south as Ban Ma Thuot

B4 Front covered I Corps north of Da Nang

B5 Front immediately south of the DMZ

Full orders of battle for the Tet Offensive are difficult to ascertain so what follows is a list of units engaged in the main battles;

The Demilitarized Zone

The siege of Khe Sanh; 304th, 308th and 325C NVA Divisions

Quang Tri Province; 812 NVA Regiment, 324B Division

The battle along Route 9; 320th and 324th NVA Divisions

Hue

The initial attack on Hue; 4th and 6th NVA Regiments

At least NVA three regiments were sent from Khe Sahn later

Da Nang

Battle for Da Nang; 2nd NVA Division

Saigon

5th, 7th and 9th VC Regiments took up blocking positions around the capital

C-10 VC Sapper Battalion attacked the Presidential Palace, the US Embassy and other key targets

Tan Son Nhut airbase D16 and 267th VC Battalion and one battalion of 271st VC Regiment

Cholon Districts; 5th and 6th VC Local Force Battalions

FURTHER READING

Many books and articles have been written about the Vietnam War. Professor Edwin E. Moise of Clemson University, South Carolina and Professor Jenson of the University of Illinois have compiled extensive online bibliographies. Their web pages on Tet and the Battle of Khe Sanh alone list dozens of books and articles. Their home pages are:

http://www.clemson.edu/caah/history/FacultyPages/EdMoise/bibliography.html

http://tigger.uic.edu/~rjensen/vietnam.html

General Books on the Vietnam Conflict

A to Z of the Vietnam War; Edwin E. Mose; Scarecrow Press (2005)

The Vietnam War Handbook; Andrew Rawson; The History Press (2008)

Vietnam Order of Battle, 1961–1973; Shelby L. Stanton; Stackpole Books (2003)

Books on the Tet Offensive

This Time We Win: Revisiting the Tet Offensive; James S Robbins, Encounter Books (2012)

Further Reading

Tet Offensive 1968: Turning Point in Vietnam; James Arnold, Osprey Publishing (1990)

Tet! Turning Point in the Vietnam War; Don Oberdorfer, Johns Hopkins University Press (2001)

The Tet Offensive: A Concise History; James Willbanks, Columbia University Press (2008)

The Tet Offensive; Marc J. Gilbert, Praeger (1996)

Khe Sanh: Siege in the Clouds; Eric Hammel, Pacifica Military History (May 14, 2009)

Khe Sanh, 1967–68; Gordon L. Rottman, Osprey Publishing (2005)

The End of the Line, The Siege of Khe Sanh; Robert Pisor, W. W. Norton & Co, (2002)

Marines in Hue City; Eric M. Hammel, Motorbooks International (2007)

Phase Line Green, The Battle for Hue 1968; Nicholas Warr; Naval Institute Press (2012)

The US Marines in Vietnam Illustrated Official History is available online.

US Marines in Vietnam, 1968, The Defining Year by Jack Schulimson and others, published by the Museums Division, United States Marine Corps in 1997

INDEX

Index

Index